WOMEN'S STORIES FOR GOD'S GLORY

An 8 Week Study of Old Testament and
Contemporary Women of Faith

Written by Marilyn Mitchell

authorHOUSE®

AuthorHouse™
1663 Liberty Drive
Bloomington, IN 47403
www.authorhouse.com
Phone: 1-800-839-8640

First published by AuthorHouse 9/24/2009

ISBN: 978-1-4490-1773-6 (sc)

Printed in the United States of America
Bloomington, Indiana

This book is printed on acid-free paper.

Dedication

I would not have been able to write this book without the unconditional support of my husband, Bill Mitchell, the love of my life. There would be no *Women's Stories* without his encouragement. Of course, I must dedicate this also to my dad and mom, Jack and Betty Schwanz for giving me life and all their years of encouragement and nurturing.

Table of Contents

Acknowledgments

Thank you to the many that have helped with this project. First, to the sisters in Christ whose stories are in this book: Sue Dahlmann, Ortheia Barnes Kennerly, Diane Dorcey, and Toni McIlwain for continuing to encourage me to complete this project. Susie you were always there holding me accountable week after week! Ortheia, thanks for your prayer support and words of wisdom. Thank you to Michelle Duke for sharing her missionary journey. Thank you to Randy Rubin, who is always there for me! Thanks to Marilyn Dean and June Kenny for their encouragement and editing support, and June for your graphic support. Thanks to my daughter, Eron Powers, who helped me with graphics. Thank you to Beth Jones and Michelle Snow who counseled me about publishing. Thank you to Dr. David Abbott who pointed me to Author HOUSE. Thank you to Michael Sterioff of MCS Digital, mcsdigital@gmail.com for his photo on the cover. And much thanks to sacred dancer, Kimberli Boyd from "Dancing Between the Lines" for gracing our cover. Thank you to the women who attended the pilot classes and helped me shape this study at Brighton Christian Church. Thank you to my family for hanging in there through all the years of working on this and other projects—first, my husband, Bill, and our kids: Lynne, Bob, Dave, Carol, Eron, and Amber. Thank you to our grandkids—Bobby, Kirstie, Andrew, Kaitlyn, Jonathan, and Kallie. Thank you to my Mom, Betty Schwanz and my mother-in-law, Marie Mitchell for always encouraging me. And most important, thank you to the Father God, my Lord and Savior Jesus Christ, and the Holy Spirit who inspired this project in the first place. May this be for your glory!

Purpose

The purpose of *Women's Stories for God's Glory* is to tell the stories of women who have overcome challenging life circumstances through their faith in God and in his son, Jesus Christ, and to inspire the readers to put their faith in Jesus. The book also contains stories of women of the Bible from the Old Testament and how they overcame their challenges through direct encounters with the Living God. This is an eight-week study, with an introductory session prior to the eight weeks.

Introduction

Have you ever met someone who has been through tough life circumstances and always seems to land on her feet? Have you seen that person bounce back through one disaster after the next and come out better than before? Have you found yourself relying on that person when you were walking through your own personal challenges? Did she seem to have strength in spite of what life continually doled out to her? If you looked deeply into her life, you would see it took more than just her character to get her through those tough challenges. In addition, her character had been developed through the trials.

Each of the women in this book has one thing in common. They had an encounter with the Living God and their lives were changed for eternity. Some had this faith all along, and others developed their faith in their time of need. The desperation they experienced caused them to reach deep for something more. They were not content to live life on their own terms. They had gotten to the edge of themselves and their personal philosophy of life, and found something more. For the women of the Old Testament, it was God, and for the contemporary women, his son, Jesus Christ, and the Holy Spirit. These contemporary women know they cannot live life by their own strength of character, and that it's not enough to get them through the storms of life. They each reached out to the one true God of the universe, and his living son, Jesus, to guide them through the rough waters until they land safely on the shore of heaven when their days on earth are through.

All of us know what it's like to attempt to live life on our own terms. Daily, we are surrounded by others we must answer to and interact with, whether our families, friends, co-workers, or those we encounter spontaneously. In the midst of living out our lives, we face trials and suffering as well as joy and triumph. We seek to understand how to live this life in the best way. No matter where we came from prior to entering at birth through our parents, what sustains us throughout our lives, or where we will go after our life on earth, we question if there is more than we can see with our eyes. When faced with the death or sufferings of others, we question who is behind it all. Is there a God? What is the truth? Who will help us in our time of need? Our lives are challenged; our minds are stretched to understand where we came from, where we're going, and what the true meaning of life might be.

Those who have been hurt from a young age may trust others and life so little they don't believe there could be a supreme creative being, a God who would allow such suffering to exist. How could this be? Others seek, through their pain, to reach toward God. They long for him to be real and to walk beside them through the challenges of life. All of us, no matter where we live on this earth, have a sense there is something greater than us; something from which we came and from which we were given birth. In the reality of our lives, we see our parents (those who know our birth parents) as authorities in our lives. Depending on how they treated us, we learned to trust or distrust others. We may have been taught to believe in God or whatever religious orientation our caretakers embraced. How do we live that out in our lives? Each of us has freewill to choose how we will live our lives. God created us this way. Each of us has the sanctity of our minds, no matter what external forces in our lives insist we believe.

You have this book in your hand for a reason. Someone gave it to you, you chose to purchase it, or you received it as part of a Bible study. It's filled with stories of women of the Bible from the Old Testament. It takes a Christian worldview. It was not designed to convince you that other religions are right or wrong. It is designed to share stories of women who have had an encounter with the Living God, Jesus, in the midst of living out their lives, often as they walked through challenging life circumstances. These women are either from Biblical times or from times that are more recent. The book can be read individually, or as a group. It includes questions for potential Bible study format.

It is our hope that you will find God, and his Son, Jesus, as your Lord and Savior, or that you will grow closer to Him as you read these pages and hear the inspirational stories. This book is presented for God's glory—*Women's Stories for God's Glory*.

Sharing your life story with the group using the following LifeMap

Each of us will take a turn sharing our own life's story during this course, as it relates to our walk with God. We will spend about fifteen to twenty minutes each session with a different person telling her story each week. You can approach this in several ways, but the one I like the most is to do a timeline of your life, using the LifeMap on the next page.

Note the key events of your life—where you were born, schooling, graduation, marriage, children, career changes, death of a loved one, etc. Note the key moments that relate to your walk with God—the churches you belonged to, baptism, confirmation, and commitment to Christ, along with any experiences you consider significant in finding God. No answer is wrong, and don't compare yourself to another. Each of our lives is unique, as you will see.

Simply start from birth and mark off the years of your life ending at your current age. Divide the timeline in half and fill in the years and events that you consider significant. Just doing the exercise will jog your memory. Use the example that I have provided of my LifeMap to inspire you in completing your LifeMap.

You may also write or type your story, remembering that whatever you add to your list must indicate a time sequence. Some women like to bring pictures that are significant to their story. Your group leader will be the first to share her story with you.

Women's Stories for God's Glory: LifeMap

Birth — Dec. 24, 1950, Detroit, MI, to Jack + Betty Schwonz, 5th of 10 Kids

Christmas — Singing with family — Lutheran Church — Baptized — Sunday School 5 yrs. + — Catechism classes

1965 Singing in Yard — 15 yrs.

Lutheran Church +Confirmation 1960

Graduate MHS 1969 — 17 yrs. — Left church — CMU Accepted Christ 1971 — 21 yrs. — CMU GRADUATE 1973

Fall 1969 Baptism — Search for God church

Studied other World Religions — New Age Views — Rebellion 1975 Prayer up north, told God "Reveal yourself to me." — Rejected Faith — Moved to Ann Arbor

Married to First Husband 1979 — 28 yrs. — UNITY CHURCH 1979 — Eron's Birth 1979

Left Unity, god of own life... — Head of Sunday School 1981 — Amber's Birth 1981

Divorce 1989-90 — Church Search Met Bill — Looking for Jesus + — Married Bill July 1993 New family — LYD '91-99 Read Bible 1994 cover to cover

Brighton Christian Church 2001-2004 — RiverEdge 1st Pres. Healing — Call to Seminary — JOURNEY ATS 1995 +Cornerstone — Recommitted Life to Christ, '95

Celebrate Recovery Codependency 2001-2004 — Missions Ethiopia, Nicaragua, Tanzania 2002-2007 2003-2009 — Women's Stories for God's Glory 2004-2009 — BCC WMT Leader 2006-2009

Present Time — June 30, 2009

Women's Stories for God's Glory: LifeMap

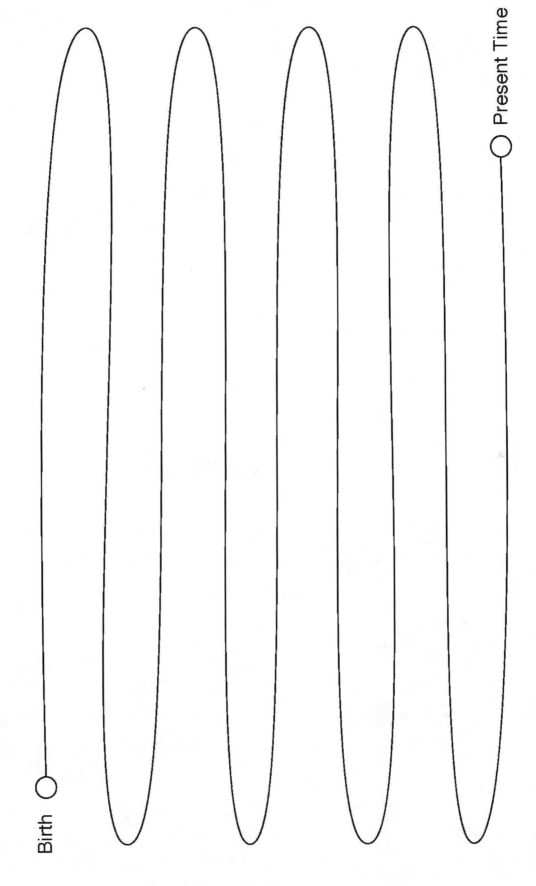

Birth

Present Time

Chapter One: In the Beginning!

There is always a starting place; some event or recorded incident from which we begin. Where did the first woman's story start? History started out as an oral tradition. Generation after generation passed on the stories of their people. In time, those stories were written down. The first mention of women in the Bible is in Genesis 1: 27. We read, "In the image of God he created them, male and female." The first woman we read about in the Bible is Eve. According to the word, Eve came from Adam's rib (the first man), and was made as a suitable helpmate for him, because it was not good for him to be alone. And the man and the woman became one flesh, joined together by God, and created by him.

We all know that one of Eve's first recorded acts was to interact with the serpent, be tempted by him, and choose to eat the fruit of the tree of knowledge of good and evil, and then offer it to Adam who also ate. God told Adam they were to stay away from the fruit of this tree. If you are someone who is not familiar with the Bible, many questions may come up for you about this story. I challenge you to take a deeper look into this story and its personal meaning for you. There was always something missing to me about this guilt-laden story of the two of them disappointing God and then being punished. I really didn't get it. Over time, I've received further information about this story, and I've started to understand.

Imagine you were the first created woman in paradise with the first created man. Everything's available; no problems exist; intimacy with God exists, and all is well, except for a snake that comes into in the garden. Then there's the tree that we're not supposed to eat of the fruit, and the challenge that the snake throws down to eat some fruit of the tree of knowledge of good and evil. What is this tree, anyhow, and how come we can't touch it? This doesn't seem to make sense. Everything else is taken care of. Why does God seem to know about good and evil, and what does he know that we don't? Why do we have to follow this one rule?

It's clear from the beginning. God created us with the ability to choose, or we'd just be robots answering to God exactly as he would have us do. All is not well in paradise, because we can choose to eat this fruit or not. We're being tempted by this snake that seems pretty shady to us. Author Erwin McManus, in his book *Uprising*, shares these thoughts about this incident.

"Adam and Eve's birthright was a life of freedom and pleasure. Yet with so much to discover, so much to experience, and so much opportunity, they chose to hang around the one tree bearing the one fruit that was forbidden them." (1)

How much is this like life today? As children, most, but not all, have it pretty easy. We cry and we are either fed, changed, rocked, and comforted. Life seems like paradise as children. Some children are born into difficult situations from the start. Their life is one of great pain and suffering from the beginning.

For the most part, children are precious to their parents and life is paradise for them. This was true for me. I was born into a wonderful family to my parents, Jack and Betty. I was the fifth of what eventually became a ten-sibling family (six boys and four girls). I grew up having a lot of attention from my older sisters, brothers, Mom, and Dad. Mom says that I was a happy baby who cried very little. I was surely loved, as were all my brothers and sisters. Mom and Dad made sure I knew about Jesus by sending my siblings and me to the local Lutheran church. I loved singing "Jesus Loves Me" in my Sunday school classes. I sang "Away in a Manger" at the top of my little lungs with my brothers and sisters with the tender heart of a child at Christmas time.

Yet, I had a mind of my own. Sounds a little like Eve? I remember my dad calling me bullheaded when I was a kid. I guess that meant I was strong willed. I was determined to do things my own way. In high school, I poured that determination into activities, such as working after school, attending a special honors program, being in choir, involved with the school plays, being president of the Student Council, and attempting to do good things with my life. During my freshman year in college, I attended an Assembly of God church. When asked if I wanted to receive Jesus, I immediately went up to the altar. The next week I was baptized by immersion and that was the extent of my experience with the church. A girl in my dorm attempted to talk to me about her family members and her concern that they be saved. Just the language turned me off. I continued to read the Bible on my own, looking for positive verses that I could understand. I went in and out of churches that required little of me. Since my family had pretty much quit the church scene due to an abusive pastor at our primary church, there was no one looking over my shoulder to encourage me to seek God through organized religion.

I went through a rebellious period as a young adult. I graduated from college in 1973, just after the war in Vietnam. At that stage of life, I rejected the notion of church, even though I had attended many church services in college. Part of my liberation was to study other world religions such as Hinduism, Buddhism, and Zen philosophies. I rejected the notion of church, not having had a positive experience as a child.

A couple of people tried to get me to explore a relationship with Jesus. A man who lived across the street from me was open about his walk with God, and encouraged me to consider seeking Jesus. He likely saw through my situation and wanted to help. At the time, I wasn't very receptive.

One of my first jobs out of college brought me in contact with a PhD who had a deep faith and read the Bible at lunch every day. He encouraged me to read the Bible. I didn't understand this book at all and was more interested in pursuing my own path in life. Deep inside, I was in pain and nothing seemed to fill the hole in me. I was in a six-year relationship with someone I thought I'd marry. I ended the relationship when it appeared we were never going to marry. I was still searching for the man of my dreams when I met my first husband. Within a year, we were married.

Somehow, entering the ranks of the married caused me to wake up. I started seeking God in a new way. I went to local churches, which led us to the church that became our home for several years. This was a beginning of finding the one true God of the universe. In my heart,

I loved Jesus, but not the church. My daughter, Eron, was born a week after we first attended this church. I felt supported by the pastor, who promised to pray for me as I prepared to give birth.

We continued to attend the church until a new minister came, and then we left. During the years we were there, I was head of the Sunday school and my husband was head usher. The female minister believed that God would call me to become a minister. I asked her to let God lead me around this. Our second daughter, Amber, was born two years and six days after her sister. Over the years, I continued to seek God, doing it from a new age perspective. I tried to be god of my own life, but Jesus kept coming back to me. I really didn't know what it meant to be a Christian, other than what I knew as a child.

In 1986, I met a Christian minister. He explored new age thinking for awhile and then returned to his Christian faith. He was the first one to tell me that I didn't really understand who the REAL Jesus was, and that I was following a false view of God and Jesus. I resented this, but then entered a turning point in my life where everything seemed to fall apart.

My husband and I decided to divorce. This was the most difficult time of my life. There is much to our story together, and the details are not necessary to this study, but I will tell you this. We prayed God would show us how to stay together or how to let go as we faced an impasse in our marriage. Later, when I recommitted my life to Christ, and studied what the Bible has to say concerning marriage and divorce, I realized that God had no intention for our marriage to end, but that we had made that decision based on what we understood at the time. Years later, I realized how much I had hardened my heart over time in our marriage.

We decided to divorce and I began the most painful time of my life. I was a single parent to two daughters, eight and ten years old. I had just started a new business as an independent contractor doing training with major auto companies. Financially, it was the most difficult time of my life.

I was on my knees to Jesus praying for his leading in my life. Within a short time, I met Bill, the man I am married to today. As we dated, we began to search for a church that would teach us about Jesus. In many of the churches, as I heard the gospel presented, I didn't respond well to what I heard, because of the guilt I'd felt for being divorced. I had sinned in so many ways, and it was hard to face this. My new age views had allowed me to see life from a positive perspective, not having to own my shortcomings. I also found that most of the religions that I had studied taught about having to earn my way to God. For years, that was what I was attempting to do. But God was beginning to work in my life, and he was showing me a different way to live.

In time, I was led to create a program called "Living Your Dreams" with the support of my best friend, Diane. It involved setting goals and resolving painful life issues through techniques we had learned. In time, I started to accomplish many goals. Bill asked me to marry him, and I said yes. We were in love. He was divorced and both of us wanted a relationship that would last for the rest of our lives. Although he had grown children and four grandchildren at the time, he was willing to become a stepfather to my two daughters. We decided to build a house of our dreams to begin our new marriage together.

Both of us continued seeking to know more about Jesus. In 1994, I was led to read the Bible from cover to cover. It was life-changing. Through prayers of friends, I recommitted my life to Christ, and began to learn what it meant to be a true follower of Jesus Christ. In 1995, I entered seminary, which was life-changing for me. I felt God used this time to heal my relationship with the church and bring me close to him. I understood for the first time what it meant to be a Christian woman. I was overwhelmed that God could forgive me. I saw how stubborn and self-willed I had been. I saw the path of people behind me that I had hurt, especially my children. Over time, God has brought many people and situations into my life to bring about restitution, reconciliation, and restoration.

I see, similar to the description in Acts 9, when Saul was struck down on the road to Damascus to persecute early Christians and converted to Paul, the Apostle that God allowed me to be struck down in my life. I was living my own way and in need of healing. I couldn't do it on my own. I needed the love of a savior. I needed the love of Jesus. By grace, he has extended that to me. I am blessed today beyond belief. I feel there is nothing I long for more in my life than Jesus to live in me, and that I'm empty of myself. I was blind, but now I see. I am grateful to be free indeed. My husband, Bill, and I are part of a church committed to Christ. Many of our family members are Christians, and we are praying for the rest of them to be blessed by Jesus.

At times, I think some of the people in my life think my faith is just one more passing phase I am in. I see now that all roads lead to Jesus for me. There's no other road for me to take in life. I have found the living water that I sought. I have found the answer to every prayer I have ever had. I have found the peace that passes all understanding that I sought, now that Jesus lives in me. In 2000, I was re-baptized, knowing for the first time what I was doing. I died to self and was reborn in Christ Jesus. There is no greater blessing in my life.

The expression "progress, not perfection," means a lot to me. I know that Jesus is perfect and I am not. I want to become more and more like him in all aspects of my life. I seek him every day, and my life is blessed. Adam and Eve had the "perfect" relationship with God, chose to do what God said not to, and because of this, they entered the world of good and evil where pain was an everyday reality. In our era, most of us are exposed to God through an organized institution. Adam and Eve knew God intimately. When I realized I could have an intimate, personal, one-on-one relationship with God, my life was changed. All of us can relate to being children, some in idyllic environments and some not. Yet, we all fall short of what God intended us to be. We need the love of his Son to redeem us.

Perhaps you are in a situation where you are "out of paradise." You find yourself suffering from trying to do life on your own. Describe your current situation:

Scripture Study

Read the full story of the creation of Eve and the downfall of Adam and Eve. Read Genesis 2:18–25 and 3:1–24. There is much to glean from these words. What strikes you the most about these passages?

What was it that caused Eve to want to jeopardize her intimate relationship with God?

Do you have an "intimate" relationship with God and his son, Jesus? Describe your relationship at this time.

Do you find your relationship with God jeopardized at times? How?

What are the things that you can do to create or maintain an "intimate" relationship with Jesus?

What is God calling you to do at this time?

Pray to God for assistance to take the next step.

---

(1) McManus, Erwin R. *Uprising*, Nashville, Nelson Books, 2003, p. 15.

PRAYER REQUESTS:

NOTES:

Chapter Two: The Long Journey...The Birth of a Nation...Hope for the Future

If you think about it, there are many women of the Old Testament we could study. No study such as this would be complete without the story of Sarah. Sarah started out as Sarai, wife of Abram, son of Terah of UR of the Chaldeans. Abram, Sarai, and their family had moved to Haran, (a city of modern day Iraq). It was common for people to move, but this was an unusual act of obedience of God for Abram. Moving to the land of Canaan, God made a promise to Abram to bless his offspring and make a great nation of him. But there was famine in the land. Abram moved his family and their servants and livestock to Egypt.

Sarai was a beautiful woman and Abram feared for his life. He told others that Sarai was his sister so that Pharaoh would not have him killed to take Sarai as his own wife. Sarai was taken into the palace and serious diseases struck the people in Pharaoh's home. Pharaoh then challenged Abram to tell the truth, that Sarai was his wife. They were sent on their way, and moved to Mamre near Hebron.

Sarai continued to age and she had no children. The Bible says that Sarai was "barren;" Genesis 11:30. Can we all relate to this experience? Perhaps childbearing was not the issue, but maybe there has been barrenness of another form in our lives. Can we all relate to Sarai's human nature of wanting to "fix" the situation in some way; or perhaps to fill in the hole that we're experiencing in our lives?

How did Sarai attempt to fill the hole in her life? At that time, offspring, especially sons, were important to the survival of a people or a particular bloodline. Sarai, in her desperation, gave her maidservant from Egypt, Hagar, to Abram so she could bear children for him. When Hagar became pregnant, Sarai began to despise her. With Abram's permission to take charge of Hagar, she mistreated her. Hagar fled from Sarai, but in time, she came back and gave birth to Ishmael, Abram's first son, when he was eighty-six. Imagine how Sarai must have felt, even though she created the situation in the first place.

Then God made a deep covenant with her husband and their names were changed. He became Abraham, meaning "father of many," and she became Sarah, still meaning "princess." God told Abraham He would bless Sarah with a son at the age of ninety. Imagine that! He would name him Isaac. Sarah overheard three men of God talking with Abraham and laughed to think she would have a child long past her childbearing years. How could this be?

Yet, she did have a son and he was named Isaac, meaning, "he laughs," because both Abraham and Sarah laughed to think God could give them a son so late in life. How many of us would have given up on a dream for our lives long before Sarah did? God had promised he would make a great nation of both Abraham and Sarah. All of us can relate to having a call on our lives of some kind, whether it's a natural call as a woman to marry, have children, or in modern times, to have a career. For those of us who love God, we turn to him for direction in our lives.

How many of us have lost patience at times with God when the "dream," vision, or calling on our life hasn't manifested? We've heard the expression, "Hindsight is 20–20 vision." Looking back at our lives, we can see what God was doing all along, but when we are in the midst of living out our lives, we can lose faith in the journey, especially when challenges surface.

Michelle Duke believes she had a call on her life from the young age of thirteen. When she was sixteen, she was in Chiang Mai, Thailand, sleeping on a concrete floor while on a mission trip.

She was awake one night when she heard the still small voice of God saying, "Michelle, would you be willing to come back here if I asked you to?"

She answered yes. It would be eight long years before she would return with a husband and two small children. With eight years of waiting to go, they did a lot of "wandering" in the desert while waiting to hear the Lord's direction of where they would minister, when, and with whom.

Here is the story of their many years of wandering in their Abrahamic journey. After Michelle married Jeff, they went to China for three weeks to explore opportunities there. They waited a year in Michigan as was requested by their mission's team, but they were anxious to get into the field. She and Jeff gave birth to Jeremiah in 1998 after a difficult pregnancy. Shortly after, they moved to England to begin their YWAM (Youth with a Mission) training by attending a DTS (Discipleship Training School). Finally, they went to China, Thailand, and Vietnam on an outreach with their four-month-old son. They came back to the USA for three months, and then they went back to England to staff a DTS. Becoming pregnant again in 1999, they almost lost the baby. During that time, they stayed in England while waiting for the birth because of insurance reasons. God was faithful and they gave birth to a healthy baby girl, Mikayla, in their bedroom because she came so quickly!

A month later, they packed to move to Thailand. They experienced new life in a strange country that was both exciting and scary. They found a home and settled into learning the language and ministering to people in their village, especially to a woman, Tan, and her daughter, Em. Michelle wanted the whole village to know Jesus, but God asked her if she would be happy with one person if that was his will. She agreed to pray for just one and pour her life into just that one—Tan. One month later, Tan was diagnosed with HIV. Six months later, her daughter, Em, died of HIV/AIDS. God's glory filled a Buddhist temple as the Holy Spirit ministered to Tan as she lay on the floor in grief. Many felt the manifest presence of God in the room and asked about it. Jesus was introduced that day through the Thai church and lives began to change.

Tan died three months later, accepting Jesus on her deathbed. May the Lord be praised!

Just prior to that, Jeremiah was said to have a possible brain tumor. The family flew home to the USA on September 10, 2001 and the next day, 9/11 occurred. Jeff volunteered to help with the 9/11 relief work for two weeks.

Fortunately, Jeremiah did not have a brain tumor, but there were other health issues that needed to be explored, such as severe pain in his abdomen. As they investigated his condition, they moved to New York to continue helping with relief work. They were glad to help with that effort, but wanted to return to Thailand. After eight exhausting months in New York, they moved back to Michigan to rebuild relationships with the mission's team and friends. It took one year to get their support together to return to Thailand. During that time, their son, Josiah, was born in the spring of 2003. They moved back to Thailand with a clear focus on people with HIV/AIDS by doing an internship in Chiang Rai at an orphanage for children with HIV/AIDS.

Eight months later, the journey continued as they moved to Chiang Mai as their daughter, Mikayla, suffered trauma, and required intense counseling. It was one of the most difficult traumas that they had ever been through. Initially they lived with the Ridgleys, another family supported by their home church. They found a new home, and as they plugged into the community, they formed the Life Link Resource Center.

Then the tsunami came ashore in Thailand, and Jeff went to the southern coastal areas to help with relief work for two months off and on. Again, it was time to take another journey, as they came back to the USA for furlough in May of 2005. After coming to Michigan to raise funds for the next leg of their journey, they then lived in California with Jeff's parents. Again, they waited on the Lord as they worked to raise funds to return to Thailand.

While they were in the USA, their financial support was cut by half. Being exhausted and discouraged they were led by God to move to Mississippi to minister and rest for that season. After staying there for a year and a half, they came back to Michigan, awaiting a possible move to Cambodia. They did go to Cambodia for further mission work. And now God is calling them back to Thailand one more time. They have moved thirty-five to forty times over a nine year period. They know that they only have one place to lay their heads that will not be taken from them the next morning—under the shadow of the Almighty. They have given up trying to settle, because God promises that he will be with them wherever they go. And ultimately they see heaven as their home.

The moving has done one main good thing for Michelle and Jeff: Answered a prayer that Michelle has been praying for years to abide in Christ and live an abundant life. And God has provided homes and provisions for her family time and time again.

Michelle says, "We often pray that God would be brought glory through our lives, even as we sign our newsletters, 'For His glory,' and we mean it. Serving others, not looking to see what we can get, but what we can give and abiding in Christ. But the truth is that He is brought glory when we abide in Him."

Jesus said to his disciples at the last supper, "I am the vine; you are the branches. If a man remains (or abides) in me and I in him, he will bear much fruit: apart from me you can do nothing." Michelle also clings to God's word in 1 John 4:7–12, "Dear friends, let us love one another; for love comes from God. Everyone who loves has been born of God and knows God.

Whoever does not love does not know God, because God is love. This is how God showed his love among us: He sent his one and only Son into the world that we might live through him. This is love: not that we loved God, but that he loved us and sent his Son as an atoning sacrifice for our sins. Dear friends, since God so loved us, we also ought to love one another. No one has ever seen God, but if we love one another, God lives in us and his love is made complete in us."

Michelle says that she and Jeff cannot abide in Jesus if they don't love others.

Michelle says, "These kinds of situations have challenged us and made us see what is really in our hearts. Daily, in the kind of living situations we are often in, I have made a choice to take the first step in loving others first, not waiting for them to love me. I was very challenged and continue to be when having to make the first step in loving others when they don't understand or acknowledge my needs. I think it is safe to say that when we love others first then we are abiding in Christ and peace will follow. Peace is my pillow at night when I am abiding in Christ. 'Desperate fellowship with Christ and a determination to obey' is what keeps us going the course—wanting to bring glory to God as we journey with him."

Perhaps you have been in such a situation where God has you moving from place to place with a promise of a calling that he has on your life in some way. Perhaps you are currently homeless or in a transitional housing program. Perhaps he has you in the same geographical place, but change is a constant in your life. Or perhaps you are the exact opposite and you are patiently waiting as no change seems to occur in your life. Whatever the circumstance, can you relate to Sarah and Michelle?

Can you see that God is calling you to something in your life, but it hasn't manifested just yet, and your patience is wearing thin?

Scripture Study

Read about Sarai/Sarah in the following verses: Genesis 11:27–32; 12:1–20; 16:1–16; 17:15–22; 18:1–15; 21:1–7; 23:1–2.

It's evident that Sarai/Sarah got impatient waiting on God to deliver her and Abram/Abraham a child. How have you tried to take "God's plan" into your own hands while attempting to make something happen, before it's time?

Would you have the faith to wait on the Lord as Michelle is learning to do, raising three children in so many different places? What are your thoughts about this?

When Sarai had been impatient and allowed her servant, Hagar, to have a son, Ishmael, by Abram, and then mistreated her out of jealousy, can you relate to feelings of jealousy when others around you seem to have what you want, but you are not receiving?

How do Michelle's words, of her lessons of learning to love others as God has called us to love them, speak to you at this moment?

Are there others who are difficult for you to love in your life as you walk out God's call on your life?

What is God calling you to do because of this lesson?

Write a prayer to God concerning this issue.

PRAYER REQUESTS:

NOTES:

Chapter Three: A Woman's Sorrow

Is there any life that is free from sorrow? As much as we might not like it, sorrow enters all of our lives at one time or another. Joy enters our lives as well. Life is a mix of both. There are many women of the Old Testament to study. Yet, there is a continued story of Sarah and Abraham's family—the great nation that God promised to Abraham. Sarah had died. In his forties, Isaac, their son, needed a wife and Abraham wanted him to have a wife from his own tribe. He sent his chief servant to find a wife from Nahor, Abraham's brother. In Genesis 24, we read the story of the chief servant, who prayed to the God of his master to give him success. The story ended with Rebekah, the granddaughter of Nahor marrying Isaac, a man she had never seen. More times of journey for the people of God!

As her mother-in-law, Sarah had been barren; Rebekah was barren for twenty years. It must have brought her great sorrow! This was a challenging time for her. Isaac prayed to the Lord, and Rebekah gave birth to twins, Esau and Jacob. God interceded for them. There is much more to this story concerning the birthrights of Esau and Jacob and even the deception that Rebekah created around this issue for her sons. That story is for another book.

In time, Jacob left to find a wife from his mother's tribe. He fell in love with Rachel, the daughter of Rebekah's brother, Laban. We read in Genesis 29 the story of what transpired. Jacob promised to work seven years for Laban, his uncle, so he could marry Rachel. Laban tricked Jacob on his wedding night. He covered his older daughter, Leah, with a long veil and gave him to Jacob as his wife. In a week's time, Laban gave Rachel to Jacob as his wife, as well. Rachel was Jacob's favorite wife, and Leah was left out and unloved by Jacob. In the midst of deception, sorrow came to Leah who was unloved by Jacob.

Genesis 29:31 says, "When the Lord saw that Leah was not loved, he opened her womb, but Rachel was barren." Leah became the mother of six sons (Reuben, Simeon, Levi, Judah, Issachar, Zebulun), and one daughter, Dinah. Her maidservant, Zilpah, gave birth to two more sons (Gad and Asher). Rachel was barren and in grief that she could not give Jacob children. So she, like Sarah, Jacob's grandmother, gave her maidservant, Bilhah, to Jacob, who bore him two sons (Dan and Naphtali). The tribe of Israel was off and running! Ten sons for Jacob. Yet, Rachel was in sorrow for not bearing Jacob sons from her own womb. Finally, Rachel gave birth to Joseph; one who would become the pride and joy of Jacob, his father. Then she gave birth to Benjamin. Rachel died in childbirth. Sorrow and joy! Children are such a joy whether our own or someone else's children, and yet, they can bring sorrow as well.

Sue Dahlmann is someone who has known great joy as a mother and great sorrow. The following is her story.

One of the greatest joys of my life after I graduated from college was to become a second grade school teacher. I loved those little second graders. The only problem was I wanted to take them all home with me. They were just so cute, and I couldn't wait to have my own children.

Marilyn Mitchell

I wondered what my own kids would look like. My husband, Denny, and I were blessed in 1970 with our first daughter, Jennifer Noelle Dahlmann. Then our daughter, Kimberly Marie Dahlmann, was born. What a blessing. The greatest blessing of my life was to be the mother of these two beautiful children.

Something that has also been important to Sue is her relationship with the Lord. She realized she was serving the Lord, but wasn't seeking a relationship with him. She started seeking that relationship through a Bible study, and created a personal relationship with Jesus Christ for the first time. She knows now that His plan is good. She realized He was preparing her for the biggest challenge of her life.

Again, in Sue's own words, "Three and a half years ago, I found out that my precious daughter, Jennifer Noelle, had a very rare form of cancer. When my granddaughter was born, they found a fibroid cyst in Jen. She had urecal carcinoma. Only 1 in 15 million people contract this disease. It usually occurs in men over the age of sixty-five years. 'How could this be, Lord? How could this be?'"

Jen had surgery to remove the cyst at that time.

On Christmas 2003 we celebrated two and a half years of Jennifer being cancer-free. Usually this disease comes back in the first two years. So we praised the Lord. We were so grateful as a family. I said, "Thank you, God, thank you, God, thank you, God."

Jennifer wept at the table as she told us all how grateful she was that she had time to raise these two beautiful children.

On March 29, 2004, Jennifer called me. A tumor the size of lemon was in her lung. Our whole family gathered around her. We slept beside her in her bed. We took every meal to her. We just lifted her up. She had so much courage, so much faith, and so much strength. You wouldn't believe how well she came through the operation to remove the tumor and two-thirds of her lung. They said that she had to have eighteen weeks of chemotherapy. She walked through the summer every week having chemotherapy. Every week she got a clean and good strong blood scan.

One day as we were at Dr. Petrolac's office, I leaped from the chair, and said, "Jen, we're not surviving, we're thriving! We're thriving, honey."

She leaped up with me. She was so strong.

On October 14, she got a clean body scan. No cancer.

Just two days later, she called me and said, "Mom, I've got a headache and I'm losing my vision. I just want you to know that I'm going to the doctor to get it checked."

She called me that night and said, "Mom, I've got two brain tumors."

I tell you I was on my knees. I went to see her. I was there the next day. On Monday, she went into the hospital. Tuesday, she had brain surgery. Jen had chemotherapy and radiation every day for a month. Every day. God's grace went before us and carried us through every moment of that time. The more she faded away, the more grace and peace she had.

As my husband Denny and I worked through it, we were pushing her through the halls to the radiation ward of that New York hospital. Every year, my husband and I and our family vacationed in Maine.

That day my husband Denny said, "Susie, look."

On the wall of that radiation ward was a picture of a fishing boat like we would see in Maine. On the back of the boat was the name, Jenny D. As much as we didn't want to be there, we knew that we were where the Lord wanted us to be. We were walking His walk one day at a time.

Jenny D was what we called our daughter when she was young.

As Jenny finished her treatments, they found out it had gone into her spine.

She looked at me and said, "Mom, you've got to let me go."

I said, "Jen, we could still have a miracle."

She said, "Mom, you didn't hear me. You've got to let me go."

We brought Jen home, and a week later, she passed away. I want to read you a page from my journal.

I wrote, "Oh, God, I am not accepting my daughter's death. It feels too hard and too painful to even imagine. So, Lord, I'm begging you for my will and hoping that it also aligns with your will. I'm not trying to change your mind. But I'm trying to have my way."

I had my miracle. My miracle was Jenny. My miracle was my daughter that I got to be with for thirty-four years. God doesn't give us these problems. He gives us the strength to walk through it one day at a time. His plan is so far greater than I can even begin to see.

I remember Jen saying, "Mom, I'm leaving you a legacy. I'm leaving you Sydney and Max. Haven't I been so lucky to live for three years and see Sydney's personality in that time? This is what I have to live for."

God has given Sue both great joy and incomprehensible sorrow through the loss of her daughter.

But, as Sue said, "God doesn't give us these problems."

He does allow us to walk through times of trouble.

As she said, "He gives us the strength to walk through it one day at a time."

I had the blessing to walk alongside Sue during Jenny's illness. I saw Sue grow stronger in her faith, and she knew that others were praying for her and her family. All of us walk through challenging life circumstances. We deal with loss in our lives through many situations—loss of love, death of others, changes that occur every single day of our lives, and sometimes grief beyond belief.

But as Jesus said to his disciples shortly before he went to go to the cross and his death, "In this world you will have trouble. But take heart! I have overcome the world." John 16:33 (NIV)

It's hard to hear stories of sorrow and not feel our own grief. Have you faced great sorrow in your life? Or has sorrow touched someone else you have known? Tell us about it.

Scripture Study

Read the following scriptures: Genesis 29, 30:1–24; 35:16–20. How do you think Leah dealt with her sorrow of being unloved by Jacob?

How did Rachel deal with the fact that she was barren?

Is there ever such a thing as a perfect life free from sorrow?

What lessons have you gleaned from Sue and the way that she walked through the illness of her daughter?

How will this help you grow in your faith in the Lord through sorrow?

What is God calling you to do in regards to sorrow that may have crept into your life in some way?

Write a prayer to God to guide you to take the next steps in this process.

PRAYER REQUESTS:

NOTES:

Chapter Four: A Prostitute and a Saint Serve the Lord!

There are so many stories of women in the Old Testament; too numerous to cover in this study. There is one woman whose story is not only told in the Old Testament, but also in the New Testament! Rahab! In Joshua, 2, as Joshua, son of Nun, prepared to lead the Israelites into the land of milk and honey that the Lord God had promised them through Abraham and Jacob (Israel) and Moses, one woman's story comes to light. Rahab was a prostitute in the city of Jericho, whose ruins sit just seventeen miles northeast of Jerusalem today. It was an old city with high, fortified walls. Joshua sent out two spies who entered the city and came to the house of the prostitute, Rahab, a woman who was accustomed to receiving strangers who traveled through the area into her home.

The king of Jericho knew that spies had entered his city. He sent a message to Rahab to send out the men who had "come to spy out the whole land." (Verse 3). Rahab hid the men on her roof under "stalks of flax." (Verse 6). She sent the messengers on their way outside of the city to search for the spies, giving them a false leading about where they were. She could see the writing on the wall about these Israelites.

She told the Israelite spies that evening, after the messengers from Jericho had gone out of the city to search for them, "I know that the Lord has given this land to you, and that a great fear of you has fallen on us; so that all who live in this country are melting in fear because of you." (Verses 8–9). She had heard "how the Lord dried up the water of the Red Sea" (Verse 10), as they came out of Egypt and gave two kings into their hands to be destroyed. She told them again how their "hearts melted and everyone's courage failed" (Verse 11). Most importantly, she knew "the Lord (their) God is God in heaven above and on the earth below." (Verse 11)

God had broken through to Rahab, the prostitute, who hid the spies of Israel. Now, she had the wisdom to attempt to save her family in exchange for saving the spies' lives.

She said, "Now then, please swear to me by the Lord that you will show kindness to my family, because I have shown kindness to you. Give me a sure sign that you will spare the lives of my father and mother, my brothers, sisters, and all who belong to them, and that you will save us from death." (Verses 12–13).

The spies said, "Our lives for your lives!" (Verse 14).

Rahab helped them escape out of the city, after they promised to save her and all the family members. She promised that she would hide them in her house, and she would tie a scarlet cord on the window. She helped them escape.

It was exactly as the men had said when Joshua took the city of Jericho in a unique way. First, God, through Joshua, created dry land in the Jordan River for the Israelites to cross; once again performing a miracle as he had at the Red Sea with Moses. Then the army with the priests carrying the Ark of the Covenant containing the law God had given to Moses, marched around the city walls of Jericho. They marched around the town seven times when the priests blasted the rams' horns, the city walls shattered, and the army rushed in to take the city. At the end of the battle, Rahab and her family had been spared!

How did this woman, a prostitute, and a woman of ill repute survive such a situation? God uses women and men who are often out of the ordinary to accomplish his purposes. He reveals himself to those we would least expect him to use. God revealed himself to Rahab, and her life was changed for eternity. We don't know exactly what happened to Rahab after that, except that through Rahab and Salmon, Boaz was born, which eventually gave rise through their lineage to King David, and eventually to the birth of Jesus, the son of God. We can read about this in Matthew 1:1–16! A prostitute woman became someone that God could use to save his people, and she then became a wife to an Israelite, Salmon, and eventually gave rise to kings and the King of Kings—Jesus Christ! What an amazing God we have! What hope does that give us sinners who have become saints, to be used by our Lord for the work he wants to do through us?

Truly, this work is not always easy. God calls us to a life of sacrifice and service for him. Here is the good news. Jesus is always with us as we remain in him. (John 15:5.)

The next story is of a woman who is known throughout the Christian world for the way in which she served the Lord. Corrie ten Boom, a single woman of the city of Haarlem, Holland who lived with her father and sister, served the Lord in an unusual way. During World War II, the Ten Boom family hid their Jewish neighbors who were fleeing persecution by the Nazis, behind the cover of the Ten Boom Watches store.

Corrie and her family created a secret room in which to hide the Jewish people who came to their doors in the early 1940s. They, like Rahab, hid people to protect them from their enemies. Corrie and her family felt boldness and a call from the Lord to hide their neighbors to save them from a sure imprisonment, if not death. One by one, they hid neighbors and other Jewish people who arrived at their door.

Corrie said this prayer to the Lord in her heart, "Lord, Jesus, I offer myself for your people. In any way, any place, any time." (2)

One night in the early days of Germany's occupation of Holland, Corrie was in bed and heard her sister, Betsie, downstairs. She went down to see her, and when she returned to bed, she cut her finger on a ten-inch piece of shrapnel embedded in her bed. She knew she could have died had she remained in bed.

She said to her sister, "Betsie, if I hadn't heard you in the kitchen."

Her sister said, "There are no 'ifs' in God's world. And no places that are safer than other places. The center of His will is our only safety—Oh, Corrie, let us pray that we may always know it." (3)

In the end, this family could not protect themselves from prison, and for some, death. On February 28, 1944, Corrie and her family were arrested and their lives were changed. The father, a man they called the "Haarlem's Grand Old Man," died and was buried in a pauper's grave. (4) In one of the prisons that Corrie and Betsie were in, Scheveningen, Corrie was put in solitary confinement because she was ill. She could not talk to anyone, but by the grace of God, small things happened which got her through. She received a Gospel of John and kept this with her to read during the time of day when the sun would shine in the solitary window in her cell. Because she couldn't talk to anyone, she befriended a busy black ant. Eventually, there were several ants to keep her company in the cell. She appreciated the small things that were taking place in this cell, and she knew somehow that God was with her in this time of trial.

The two sisters, Corrie and Betsie, were eventually put into the Ravensbruck extermination camp in Germany; their worst fears realized. Somehow, in all the suffering they endured, there was a sweet spirit of the Lord that sustained them through this time. They again saw small things as God worked through them during their imprisonment. They were put into barracks that were flea infested. At first, they couldn't understand how they could endure such conditions, but the two sisters used the time to minister to others and to read God's word. Through this, they received strength to endure the trials they faced.

They read in 1 Thessalonians 5:18, "Give thanks in all circumstances."

They were thankful that through many searches they were able to keep a Bible with them to use to minister to others around them. They were thankful they were together in this challenging time. They realized later that the guards left them alone in their barracks because of the fleas. They were protected even by the fleas from the greater attacks of their guards. They gave thanks even for fleas!

Shortly before Corrie was released from the prison, her sister Betsie (who was very sickly) began to have visions of life after the war. Betsie told her sister that she, Corrie, would have a large house with statues, a sweeping stairway, and gardens. She shared another vision of a concentration camp that would be run by Corrie, and would become a home for those who had been warped by the war; a place for healing to take place. As she was close to dying, Betsie told her sister that she "must tell people what we have learned here. We must tell them that there is no pit so deep that He is not deeper still." (5)

Shortly after that, her sister, Betsie died. By New Year's Day, 1945, Corrie was set free from camp. In time, she returned to her hometown of Haarlem. She remembered what her sister Betsie had said about telling others what they had learned while in the camp. She began to speak to her people to tell them that joy runs deeper than despair. It was a message the people needed to hear.

In one of her talks, she met an aristocratic woman who opened her house to become the home that Betsie had seen. It was a place called Bloemendaal, where people could come to be healed of the ravages of war. It had sculptures, gardens, and a sweeping stairway, just as Betsie had described to her, as if she had seen it in advance. Corrie knew the place that needed the greatest healing was Germany. In 1946, she fulfilled her sister's vision of turning a concentration camp in Germany, Darmstadt, into a center of healing for victims of the war. Corrie ten Boom went on to travel the world as a "tramp for the Lord," sharing the message of what she had learned until April 15, 1983, her ninety-first birthday, when she went home to be with the Lord. (6)

God uses all people who open themselves up to be used by him, whether a prostitute, a watchmaker, or whatever. He wants to use us for his good. These two stories of lives that were changed by the Lord and used for his service can be an inspiration for us as well.

Read Joshua Chapter 2, 6:22–25, Matthew 1:1–16, and Hebrew 11:30–31 to learn about Rahab. How remarkable is it to you that God not only used a prostitute to assist the nation of Israel in securing their land, but that from her lineage Jesus was born? What are your thoughts about this?

Do you personally know of any woman who was used by the Lord after living a life separate from God? Tell her story here.

If God could use Rahab, he can certainly use you! Do you have faith that the Lord can use you for his purposes? In what ways has he recently used you?

Corrie ten Boom took great risks, as did Rahab to work for the Lord. Perhaps God is not calling you to be in a dangerous situation, but how might God call you to stretch your comfort zone? Has he stretched you that way in the past? Tell us about it.

Create a prayer to the Lord about the work that he may want to do through you in the days ahead:

2. Ten Boom, Corrie, *Her Story: The Hiding Place*. New York, Inspirational Press, 1995. P. 58

3. Ibid, p. 53

4. Ibid, p. 102

5. Ibid, p. 159

6. Ibid, p. 179

PRAYER REQUESTS:

NOTES:

Chapter Five: Women as Leaders in the Old Testament and Now

This subject is near and dear to the author's heart. When I was in high school, one of my math teachers asked us to think about our individual best qualities. Two things came to mind for me. First, I could relate to any group of people I seemed to come across. I wouldn't become like them, but I could see the Creator's hand in all people. The second quality was that I was a leader. My parents were both strong leaders. My father was definitely the head of the house. My mother, in his absence, ruled the roost. She was COO (chief operating officer) of our household, which included my nine siblings, my dad, and me. Not only that, she was a leader as president of the PTA at my elementary school. She has always had strong opinions about things. Just ask her today at the age of eighty-seven. No matter what, she has always honored my dad as the leader and chief decision maker in the home, but she definitely had her opinions.

Having grown up in the age of feminism, we've seen the concept of a man as the head of the household being challenged. We have also seen the disintegration of the family as women have taken on additional roles outside the home. At some level, there has been a great increase for women to express their leadership gifts, especially in the secular world. The question I ask is how can women express these gifts in a way that supports the role that God has intended for man? In recent years, the movie, *My Big Fat Greek Wedding* was released. In one of the famous scenes in the movie, the bride's mother is explaining the roles of women and men in the home. She tells her daughter that the husband is the head of the house, but that the woman is the neck, and the neck turns the head. It was great for a wonderful laugh, but also pretty true too.

The question that we will explore in our stories in this chapter has to do with how women can express their leadership gifts in conjunction with men maintaining their leadership roles. In this process, can women be an encouragement to men and vice versa, each fulfilling their God-given purpose as men and women on earth?

One of the classic leaders of the Old Testament is Deborah, the only woman judge in the Bible and a prophet of God. We read about Deborah in Judges 4 and 5 in the Old Testament.

It says in Judges 4:4–5, "Deborah, a prophetess, the wife of Lappidoth, was leading Israel at that time. She held court under the Palm of Deborah between Ramah and Bethel in the hill country of Ephraim, and the Israelites came to her to have their disputes decided."

At the time, the nation of Israel was settled into the land of milk and honey that the Lord had promised to Abraham many years before. At this time, the Israelites were being oppressed for twenty years by Sisera, commander of the army for the King of Canaan, Jabin, who had 900 chariots. The Israelites at the time were not obeying God and they were doing "evil in the eyes of the Lord" (verse 1).

You might ask why there was a woman leading Israel at the time. It seemed unusual considering that Israel was a patriarchal society.

One commentary on this states, "Deborah most likely ascended to prominence because of a power vacuum. With no male leaders stepping forward, Deborah took the initiative. Although it was rare for a woman to do what she did, there was no divine injunction against it. In fact, God blessed her for her trust in him, and the people recognized God's hand upon her." (7)

It was evident that Deborah had a close relationship with the Lord.

Deborah received a word from the Lord and sent for Barak, son of Abinoam, and told him the following in verses six and seven, "The Lord, the God of Israel, commands you, 'Go take with you ten thousand men of Naphtali and Zebulun and lead the way to Mount Tabor. I will lure Sisera, the commander of Jabin's army, with chariots and his troops to the Kishon River and give him into your hands.'"

Barak would only go if Deborah would go with him, so she agreed to go with him, but said, "I will go with you. But because of the way you are going about this, the honor will not be yours, for the Lord will hand Sisera over to a woman" (verse 9).

Two key events occurred. First, Sisera gathered his 900 chariots, many men, and drove them into the dry Kishon River bed. Then the Lord sent thunderous rain into the river, and the chariots sank in the mud that was created. Under Deborah's direction, Barak and the 10,000 men routed Sisera and the army. Sisera then fled on foot and was killed by Jael, a woman from whom Sisera had asked for water. She gave him curdled milk, a drink of royalty, and covered him to hide him. She then drove a tent stake through his temple. The Lord had certainly delivered Sisera into the hand of a woman. In Deborah's Song in Judges 5:7, she described herself as a "mother of Israel."

She said, "Village life in Israel ceased, ceased until I, Deborah, arose, arose a mother in Israel."

She then described how the Israelites had chosen new gods, disobeyed God, and described how war had come to their city gates. Then she, through the leading of the Lord, led Barak and 10,000 men to crush their oppressors.

Many times, we women who walk with God, look for the Godly examples of women who have had great faith, listened to the voice of God, and followed it into victory. Deborah and Jael, as well, were raised for such a time as the one that they lived in. Esther, described in the book of Esther in the Old Testament, is the story of an orphaned girl who rose up to be a queen and wife of Xerxes in Persia, as her exiled Israelite people were doomed to die. She helped save them from death. Her cousin, Mordecai, believed that she was raised to save her people, and that she had "come to royal position for such a time as this" (Esther 4:14). Esther risked her life to save her people.

The expression "for such a time as this" is often quoted in Christian settings to describe the timing of God's purposes in using us for his good, AND in his timing. These women leaders can give courage to those of us who long to express our gifts of leadership for God's glory!

One of my good friends, Ortheia Barnes Kennerly, is a woman who is raised for such a time as this. Her story is an inspiration to those of us who feel a calling on our lives by God to express our leadership skills. The following is her story in her own words.

All the money I desired…living good…driving good…looking good…and dying inside, yet having a calling on my life. This is when I hit rock bottom. I had all these things and I was dying inside. I had lost what God had given me since the beginning of time. I had lost the seed of possibility and that was God's love. I found I had lost what God had given me when God said, "Let us make man in our likeness and our image, and let them have dominion over every creepy thing that creepeth upon the earth" (Genesis 1:26). I had not taken dominion over all the creepy things on this earth or in this life. I found myself with a $400,000 valued nightclub closing, a singing career at a stall, and having to file for divorce. I had always loved men more than I loved God or myself, even when men treated me badly. The next two years were an up-and-downhill journey of growing more in the Word of God and praying to become more intimate with God even while feeling sorry for myself. Here I was with the call and having no income, and no one to love, so I thought.

I found myself with no food to eat and I heard God say, "Fast. Pray and seek ye first His Kingdom and righteousness and all these things shall be added unto you" (Matthew 6:33). "Therefore do not worry about tomorrow for tomorrow will take care of itself. Each day has enough worry of its own" (Matthew 6:28).

My phone had been cut off, and I could hear God say, "Be quiet."

Then they came and took my car away.

I heard God say, "Be still, and know that I AM God" (Psalms 46:10). I found myself in the worst battle of depression I had ever been in, since fighting depression for the last four years of my life.

I had no charge or dominion over my creepy things (worry, fear, doubt, and forgiveness), yet I found God saying, "Trust in me with your whole heart and lean not to your own understanding and in all your ways acknowledge me and I will direct your path" (Proverbs 3:5).

I had to repeat this over and over again until it had taken root within my spirit and my soul. I had to totally depend and trust in God.

I finally said, "I give God, I give!"

I surrendered on my knees. I surrendered my all to Jesus. I had to really understand that He is Alpha and Omega, the beginning and the end. My family and friends became upset with me for not asking for assistance or shelter. Yet, I found in the midst of all the challenges, God provided me with a way out of no way. It wasn't the way I was used to living because I never knew what it was like to have no income, no food, to have no transportation, and then be confined to quarters like living in a convent. But here I was and I had to lean on God and trust more every day and become more intimate with God.

I finally answered God's call, "Come unto me of you who are heavy laden and I will give you rest" (Matthew 11:28). I found a peace within my spirit that passed all understanding. I finally found the answer to my peace and love. The more I fell in love with God, the more I fell in love with myself. I felt a freedom and peace that I had never felt in my life. I let God become all in all to me.

God said, "Be fruitful and multiply," (Gen. 1:22). After understanding that, God ordered my steps and He became my true husband in the Spirit. He sent me someone to love in the flesh and spirit. He sent me a great man of God, my husband, Robert Kennerly. Oh, God is good!

God ordained us to be together so that we would carry out God's plan of SpiritLove Ministries, International, where our mission was to "Know your Spirit through Love. This Love is defined by God's Love plus Christ's Love equals Corporate Love." Our ministry was a church without walls. We welcomed people regardless of race, creed, color, or denomination. We both realized that when you love God more than you love man, God will give you a permanent love for others. We fell in love with each other, but we fell more in love with God. Because we learned the more we loved God, the more we loved man. He gave us all the love we needed to love ourselves and to love someone else. What greater love is there than to love God as He loves you? So I thank God for the seed of possibility which is love that he gave back to me. There is a seed of possibility in each and every one of you. God bless you.

Ortheia is daily walking out her calling on her life, and in recent years, that has meant running for the Detroit City Council. She completed the primary in August 2005 where she passed the test, and she then campaigned for the November 2005 election in Detroit. Although she lost, she touched many lives in the process. How does a sixty-one-year-old grandmother who was once homeless have the courage to run for a political office for the first time in her life? The answer is she felt a calling by God to do this. She is a leader gifted by the Lord. Each day she spoke to numerous people in senior centers, churches, and community centers, and God is at the center of everything she does. Since the election, she has worked on other campaigns and spawned the "I Believe Ministries" that supports local non-profit groups that serve the community on the east side of Detroit. She ministers to local and state level government officials, doing her best to keep them focused on God. She knows he is the Alpha and Omega, and that he is the one who gives her the faith to walk out this calling on her life.

Perhaps God has not called you to run for a public office, or to be a queen, or a judge to lead your people. Perhaps God has another calling on your life for the leadership gift to be expressed. Perhaps you are someone who is coming alongside another woman or man who has this gift and feels the call to express it. Either way, we can learn from both Deborah and Ortheia.

Having a close working relationship with the Lord is key. Neither Deborah, Ortheia, nor even Esther was doing this from an earthly vision, but a God-led vision. They daily turned their lives over to the Lord to guide, direct, and lead. Earthly leadership is nothing without Godly leadership at the center of it, for men or women. How do these women honor men in leadership roles? Deborah believed that men should lead, and that women lead in their absence, or as gifted by God. Ortheia came from a more African-American, matriarchal culture and has naturally felt called to leadership. She and her husband, Robert, continue to work at finding balance in their family roles. Each uses their gifts to serve, as God calls them to do so.

Read Judges 4 and 5 and the story and song of Deborah. What was the condition of the Israelite nation at that time?

What do you think happened that there were no men to lead the nation?

Why do you think that Deborah was raised up as a leader by the men at that time?

How did Deborah see herself at that time?

Any other insights that you have received from this reading?

After reading Ortheia's story, does she appear as a likely candidate to lead a ministry or to run for office after what she's been through? What insights do you have from reading Ortheia's story?

We are all leaders, whether of our own kitchens or of some area of our lives. Is God calling you to express leadership skills in any part of your life? If so, what?

Do you ever find yourself thinking that you can do a leadership task better than a man around you? If so, how do you handle that situation? What is the godliest way that you can encourage the men around you to express the natural leadership that God has given to them?

What is God asking you to do with greater faith and excellence? Does it require taking a leap of faith? If so, please describe what he is calling you to do.

Write a prayer to the Lord for his grace to risk taking this leap of faith for him.

---

7. *The Quest Study Bible*, NIV, Grand Rapids, Michigan, Zondervan, p. 324.

PRAYER REQUESTS:

NOTES:

Chapter Six: Resourceful Women...Then and Now

We can't always determine what kind of circumstances we will find ourselves in as women, or as men for that matter. The question we will explore in this chapter centers around our walk of faith. How resourceful can we be in the midst of living out the challenges we face? There are multiple Biblical stories of women who have walked through danger, despair, drought, and circumstances that could cause their demise. Queen Esther (Book of Esther), whom we spoke about in the last chapter, would have experienced the demise of her people and probably herself, had she not used wisdom. The Widow of Zarephath (1 Kings 17:8–24), who faced drought and possible starvation for her and her son, had faith and demonstrated hospitality towards the prophet Elijah. She was rewarded with food for her kindness.

Bathsheba (2 Samuel 11) was taken by King David, although she was married to Uriah the Hittite, and became pregnant. She suffered not only the loss of her husband, due to David's act of having him killed, but also the loss of her first child with David, who died soon after his birth. She did her best to be obedient to the Lord, and she gave birth to Solomon, David's successor. The Lord rewarded her after she suffered such grief.

One of the most resourceful women described in the Old Testament was Abigail. Her story appears in 1 Samuel 25:2–42. She was the wife of a very wealthy, yet not very intelligent, man—Nabul. We have no description of how the very intelligent Abigail became Nabul's wife. Was she given to him by her father, who saw the wealth of Nabul and assumed intelligence? We don't know for sure, but we do know how the rest of the story played out. David, who eventually became king of Israel, had become the neighbor of Nabul and Abigail near the Desert of Maon. He, along with his six hundred men, was fleeing from King Saul, who wanted to kill him. David's presence had kept thieves from robbing Nabul of his flocks, and Nabul experienced an increase in his wealth.

David sent messengers to ask Nabul to provide provisions for his men because he had protected Nabul's flocks. Nabul, the fool, refused to give anything to David. After a servant told Abigail what had happened, she acted quickly. She was wise enough to know that David and his men would attack them and take everything that they had for the insult. This is the resourceful part. Abigail told her servants to load up donkeys with 200 loaves of bread, two skins of wine, five dressed sheep, toasted grain, and cakes of raisins and pressed figs. She then went with the food to intercede on behalf of her family.

She stepped off her donkey and bowed down to David, saying, "My Lord, let the blame be on me alone. Please let your servant speak to you." (Verse 25:24)

She proceeded to ask David to receive her apology for what had happened. She offered him all she had prepared for him and his men. David let her know that had she not interceded, not one of anything belonging to Nabul would have survived their attack on them. He graciously received what she offered and went on his way.

He said, "Go home in peace." (Verse 25:35)

When Abigail returned home, she told Nabul what had happened. He had a heart attack and, ten days later, died. When David heard what had happened, he praised the Lord, who had upheld him in the presence of a man who had insulted him. Then the most remarkable thing occurred.

"Then David sent word to Abigail, asking her to become his wife." (Verse 40)

Abigail agreed to this and became David's third wife.

How many of us would have acted so resourcefully in the face of danger? Surely, Abigail dreaded her life with Nabul but tried to make the most of the situation. How many women have found themselves in marriages that were less than they had dreamed about? Perhaps physical, verbal, or emotional abuse was part of their everyday life.

The following story highlights a woman who experienced great abuse at the hand of her first husband. She did all that she could until she couldn't take it anymore.

Many people in the community of Detroit know Antoinette (Toni) McIlwain as the president of Ravendale Community, Inc., a woman committed to assisting those who are in poverty make a positive change in many different areas of their lives. They see her as this jolly, happy person. However, she would tell you she never forgot where she came from. She has gone through a lot. She came from a family of eight. She is the oldest and has an identical twin sister three minutes younger than her. She was raised on welfare. Her mother struggled to take care of eight kids. She remembered one day when her younger sister had a child at thirteen years, and the welfare department came to take the child.

Her mother asked if she could keep the child, and they said, "No, you are on welfare. You don't have enough money, and you cannot even adopt your own grandchild."

In Toni's own words, "I remember my mother raising her fist, and saying, 'One day I am going to be somebody!'"

This is the story in her words.

I remember her struggling as she signed up for nursing school. I remember days that we were cold because we had to turn off the heat in the house to pay for her books and uniform. I remember the strength in this lady, but you know what? I ended up in the same predicament as my mother. I ended up with four kids by the time I was nineteen years of age. During my third pregnancy, I married their father. Because I was looking for something, I was really looking for love that I thought I didn't have. I began to take a lot of abuse from this man. I took abuse where my leg was broken and my jaw was wired shut. There were many times I woke up and wondered why I was taking this. I'm sure there are many of you reading this that have taken the same abuse. Here I was trapped, with no income of my own. I had dropped out of school in the ninth grade to have my first child. I had become a woman with no education with four kids. I thought no one would want us, but this abusive man.

I remember lying on the bed one day and my husband was upset because I had left the top off the ketchup bottle. Sometimes you just get tired.

I remember him pulling the rifle off the shelf after we argued and him saying, "B----? Are you ready to die?"

I said, "Yes, I'm ready to die."

I was tired, and at that point, I did want to die. I felt I had no one looking out for me. Surprisingly, he pulled the trigger! The bullet grazed my head. I pulled myself up. He left the house. I went out on the porch and collapsed. An elderly lady across the street called EMS.

When I woke up in the hospital, I said to myself, "Something has to change."

When I healed from that, my activity was to bathe the two boys, and the next day, bathe the two girls. One day, when I called my kids into the house, I decided that I had to leave home. I had only been in Detroit for one year. I had no real friends, no real neighbors, and I decided I had to leave. I told them we were leaving. They were small and we walked and walked. I literally did not know where I was going.

One of my kids asked me, "Mommy, when are we going to get there?"

How can you tell them when we're going to get there, when you have no idea where you're going? Fortunately, God sent this lady down the street with a car. She saw me out there crying, and the tears flowed.

I said, "Please, lady, can you help me?"

She put us in the car and took us to her home. She began to ask me a lot of questions, such as, "Do you drink, pop pills, or smoke?"

I said, "No, all I do is stay home, clean the house, and take care of my kids."

Little did I know that she was an ex-prostitute. She took me to her house and I noticed that she had her lights hooked up illegally, and her gas was hooked up illegally. All she would do was borrow $3.07 so she could buy a pint. She would get drunk every night. To pay her back, I would scrub the floors, clean the house, take care of my kids, and her two kids. Then one day the house caught on fire because she had the lights on illegally. She left me in the house with my four kids. I was living in an abandoned home, and every day I would go out there and search for food to feed my kids. I used to go to the stores and beg for food. I'd ask for noodles and neck bones so that I could just feed my kids. You see, noodles and neck bones go a long way. Every once in awhile they would give me food. I remember they would write the price down and put it under the cash register. I remember that I would tell them that one day

I would pay them back.

Once in a while I would walk twelve miles to borrow money from the only people that I knew so I could feed my kids. As my weight began to drop and my hair began to fall out, all I wanted to do was feed my kids. I remember seeing the veins pop out on their necks because they were so hungry. One day in my house shoes (slippers), because my shoes had worn out, and wearing an old sweater, I went to one of the stores where I had gotten food before. I pulled the handle on the door and it was closed. My kids were waiting for me to bring food to them, and I wondered, why is this store closed? Then it dawned on me. It was Thanksgiving.

I remember saying to myself, "Everyone is eating turkey, but my kids."

All I wanted to do was feed my kids turkey for Thanksgiving.

I thought to myself, when your stomach is empty, your mind doesn't think right. I thought, if I go around the end of the alley, maybe the store owner had thrown some food away. I'm thinking that I could find some food in the dumpster and wash it off. My kids wouldn't even know. Just let me find some food in the dumpster in the alley. So I proceeded to go around to the back and I looked for some food in the dumpster. That's when this big rat jumped out at me. He looked at me as if to say, "Ha ha, you're nothing but a dummy. I got the food before you did."

As I looked at that rat running down the alley, I dropped to my knees and said to God, "Lord, just open up one door for me, and I will give back the rest of my life. Just help me feed my kids."

At that time, I was truly at the end of the road.

Toni didn't stay at the end of the road. Like Abigail, who almost lost her life in addition to her family's lives, Toni became resourceful. That day in the alley, she realized she couldn't stay where she was. She got a job and eventually went back to school. In time, she met the man who would become the husband she is married to today, Roger McIlwain. Now, with her children raised, she has accomplished remarkable things with her life. She is one of the most resourceful women I know. The expression, "When life gives you lemons, make lemonade" fits well for Toni. She is constantly in challenging circumstances as the leader of Ravendale Community, Inc., where she is president. She has created a center that has housed many things—a Work First program based on "Living Your Dreams," co-authored by Diane Dorcey and me; a GED program; a computer training program; Weight Watchers; an after-school tutoring program; a senior program; and a church. There are moments when it's challenging to pay the bills for this building, but Toni keeps on keeping on with her faith that the Lord will bring her through.

As she said in the prayer in that alley, "Lord just open one door for me, and I will give back the rest of my life," she is still giving back. Many women and men who come to the center for assistance have stories similar to Toni's. She is a role model for them. "Falling in the water won't kill you; it's staying there that will." That's another "Toniism." I never cease to be amazed at how many women and men make a decision to "seek first the kingdom of heaven." They know the secret that "all these things will be given you as well" (Matt. 6:33). The Lord wants to supply us with all manner of good things and resources to fulfill the work that he longs to do through us. God wants us to use wisdom to see through the tough situations we face and find the resources to accomplish what only he can do through us. Toni, like her twin sister, Bernadette, has won many awards for the work of compassionate ministry that she has done in her community. A long wall in her center carries the frames of the many awards, but Toni always says she wishes money would accompany all those plaques so she could further fund the work she is called to do. Somehow, God usually provides Toni with what she needs to do the work.

Read 1 Samuel 25:2–42. What surprised you the most about this story of Abigail, Nabul, and David?

Why do you suppose that Nabul had a heart attack and died ten days later?

Would you have had the resourcefulness to load up all the food on donkeys and go meet David on the road, knowing that you might die along the way?

What foods would you have prepared for a future king and six hundred men to appease them?

Can you imagine fleeing from an abusive marriage with four young children and no thought about where you were going, other than to get away?

What would you have done if you were in that situation?

Are you surprised at the outcome of Toni's story and all the successes she has had, to become a role model for others in similar situations? What are your thoughts?

Have you ever been in a situation that required you to be resourceful under a potentially life-threatening situation?

In Toni's most challenging situation, she turned to God in prayer. Do you turn to God first in prayer when you are stretched to the max, or do you try to figure things out on your own first?

Write a prayer here about a current minor or major situation that you or someone near you is facing that requires an extra dose of God's infinite resources, especially his grace and mercy!

PRAYER REQUESTS:

NOTES:

Chapter Seven: Where You Go, I Will Go

Perhaps one of the most surprising women of the Old Testament is Ruth and the wonderful relationship she had with her mother-in-law, Naomi. So this lesson is a two-fer: two Old Testament women for the price of one reading.

When my dear friends Randy and Craig Rubin were married in front of the fireplace of Randy's home under the Jewish chuppah adorned with flowers, their Rabbi shared from the classic scriptures of the Book of Ruth, and it touched me deeply. As a result, when Bill and I got married, we also included the same scriptures from Ruth.

This is the story. Naomi, an Israelite woman lived with her husband, Elimelech, in Bethlehem, and when famine hit, they headed to Moab, where Elimelech died. Their two sons married two Moabite women, Ruth and Orpah. Then the two sons died, and she beckoned her daughter-in-laws to return to their mother's homes. She knew she had nothing to offer them; no more sons for them to marry. Orpah returned to her mother's home, but Ruth could not leave Naomi.

She said these classic words to Naomi, "Where you go, I will go, and where you stay, I will stay. Your people will be my people and your God, my God. Where you die, I will die and there I will be buried. May the Lord deal with me, be it ever severely, if anything but death separates you and me" (Ruth 1:16–17).

Ruth returned to Bethlehem with Naomi with no knowledge of where life would lead her. It must have been that Ruth saw the wisdom of her mother-in-law and something special about her God, the God of Israel. When Naomi, along with Ruth, returned to Bethlehem, the women of the town were surprised to see her.

They said, "Can this be Naomi?" (Ruth 2:19).

Naomi told them to no longer call her by her name, but by Mara, which meant "bitter." She said this because she had suffered so much loss.

However, all was not lost. Ruth was a wise woman and went to the barley fields to glean, or pick leftover grain behind the harvesters. To hers and Naomi's surprise, she had gone to the fields of "a man of good standing," Boaz, a relative of Elimelech. These two women were about to have their fortunes turned. Boaz came to greet the harvesters in his field and noticed Ruth. He asked the foreman who she was, and was told she was Naomi's daughter-in-law, Ruth. Boaz beckoned Ruth to continue to work in his fields, stay with his servant girls, and take water from the jug when she needed it. He told her the men would not harm her and that she would be protected. Ruth asked what she had done to deserve such kindness. Boaz told her that he had heard about her great kindness to Naomi—how she had left her biological family to come back with Naomi. She was offered the opportunity to eat a meal with them. At the end of the day, she took the grain and some of the leftover meal back to Naomi. Naomi was excited that Ruth had been harvesting in Boaz's field.

Naomi then hatched a plan with Ruth and this man who was a kinsman-redeemer. A kinsman-redeemer has three functions in a family—to protect the widow of a deceased relative; to purchase the widow's freedom; and if necessary, to marry her to carry on the family name. Naomi guided Ruth in the rituals and customs of their people. She told Ruth to wash and perfume herself and put on her best clothes. She then directed Ruth to go to the threshing floor, where Boaz would be winnowing barley. She was to wait until he had finished eating and drinking. When he was lying down, she was to uncover his feet and lie down. Naomi then told Ruth that Boaz would tell her what to do.

Ruth was willing to follow her mother-in-law's lead and went to the threshing floor. At the appropriate time, she lay down by the feet of Boaz. In the middle of the night, he awakened.

When he asked who she was, she said, "I am your servant, Ruth. Spread the corner of your garment over me since you are a kinsman-redeemer" (Ruth 3:9).

Boaz was honored that such a young woman would show him such kindness, and that she wasn't running after younger men. He knew she was a "woman of noble character" and recognized the traditions of his tribe. He explained to her that there was another kinsman-redeemer next in line to care for her and Naomi. He told her he would check with him first, and if he didn't take responsibility, Boaz would act as the kinsman-redeemer. He beckoned her to stay there the rest of the night but to leave in the morning before anyone would see her there. He filled her shawl with barley to take home.

Ruth returned home to Naomi and told her everything. Naomi knew that Boaz would take immediate action to resolve the situation. Boaz did just that. He went to the town gate and found the other kinsman-redeemer and ten of the elders of that town. He explained everything to them. The other kinsman-redeemer said he could not take the responsibility. Boaz stated publicly that he would buy the land that belonged to his brother, Elimelech. He told them that he would care for Naomi and take Ruth as his wife to provide offspring for this family line. The elders blessed him and prayed that Ruth would be blessed like Rachel and Leah and that his family would be like that of Perez, whom Tamar bore to their ancestor, Judah.

The blessing came upon Ruth and Boaz, and she conceived a son, Obed. Naomi had the joy of a "son" to hold in her lap. This grandson of Naomi, Obed, became the father of Jesse. Jesse was the father of David, the same David who later became king and gave rise from his lineage to Joseph, father of Jesus. Hallelujah!

What a blessing that not only do we have the story of Ruth, who displayed such love for her mother-in-law and respect for her God, but that we also get a window into the history of the same tribe that eventually gave birth to Jesus. How powerful are the stories preserved for us in the Bible, and oh, how they give us insight into the workings of our Lord through the nation of Israel.

Are there modern-day Ruths? Are there widows who are loyal to their former mother-in-laws? If so, how does God figure into these stories? One such story didn't require this widow to journey to a distant land with her mother-in-law, but this story does involve the same God of the Israelite women and his son, Jesus.

Diane Dorcey is a woman who became a widow at a young age, just shortly after her mother-in-law, Felicia Szymanski, lost her husband. He was in his fifties when he died. Diane has never forsaken her relationship with her mother-in-law. The following is Diane's story, and although there was not a kinsman-redeemer in the traditional sense in her life, her story has a happy ending. Read Diane's story in her own words.

Has life ever been so painful to you that you didn't want to be here or that suicide was an option? Well, it was for me. I was fourteen years old when I met the young man I was going to marry and have children with. His name was Pat Szymanski. He lived two blocks from my home in Dearborn, Michigan. We dated for seven years and married when I was twenty-one and he was twenty-two.

Diane had grown up in the Macedonian Orthodox Church but had also attended many Protestant churches as a child. She wanted to follow the religion of her future husband, Pat, and became a Catholic before they married. She even became a catechism teacher.

After they were married, they began to grow a family. Diane tells us, "God blessed us with two beautiful daughters, Lia and Brienne. I was totally in love with this man. We had a sweet marriage. My mother, Zoya, became ill with strokes that incapacitated her. It was painful to have my mother put into a nursing home when our daughter, Brienne, was only three months old.

My mother told my sisters and me, "Whatever you girls do, do not put me in a nursing home."

It was the most devastating event in my life at that time.

Three months later, in January 1979, came an even more devastating event. My husband of almost ten years told me he didn't love me anymore and wanted to separate. I felt like my heart had been broken. What could I do to go on? You can imagine how I felt after spending seventeen years of my life with him and having a six-month-old daughter. We had been separated for ten weeks, during which time we had our tenth wedding anniversary.

He wrote me a note saying, "Thank you for the love that you've given me, and thank you for spending over half of your life with me. Thank you for our two beautiful daughters."

A few weeks later, Pat asked me for a divorce. I was stunned, shocked, and in disbelief! Pat stayed until March 17. That evening, we were supposed to go out for the evening. Lia had been at a carnival with her friend and was coming in through the front door as Pat was leaving us through the back door. She ran after him and asked if she could go with him.

He said, "No. *"*

I was a Montessori preschool teacher at the time, and I had a conversation with one of my co-teachers.

I said, "I must get this in its proper perspective. After all, I could be a paraplegic! I am healthy, and my children are healthy. Many women have gone through divorces."

The next night I was awakened by a knock at the door at 4:00 a.m.

My friends were at the door and said, "Pat has been in a serious accident up north, and the doctors need your permission to operate."

My first thought was, "This will knock some sense into him and he'll come back to us."

I called the hospital and gave them permission to operate. We proceeded to go to Grand Rapids to the hospital.

The doctor said, "Your husband has two back injuries, a broken back, and a severed spinal cord. He's a paraplegic."

My mouth dropped open since I had just said those words the day before. The doctor proceeded to tell me, "Worse than that, his brain is severely damaged, and he will probably never be normal again."

I was thirty-one years old and more stunned than I had ever been! Pat was in a coma for three months, followed by going into a closed-head-injury facility in Detroit for three months. It was a long thirteen months of raising my young daughters, visiting my mother in one nursing home, and visiting my husband, Pat, in another nursing home a few miles away. Pat died June 29, 1980, after the final six months in a nursing home."

Afterwards, I took the Dale Carnegie course and it was so powerful. I was a housewife and a preschool teacher. I discovered things about myself through this situation that gave me strength. God gave me the strength to raise my daughters for twenty-one years while going back to school to finish my bachelor's degree at the University of Michigan in Dearborn. I became a Dale Carnegie instructor. He was my partner. God carried me as I journeyed through twenty-one years of teaching more than five thousand students. It was around that time when I met my dear friend Marilyn and we co-created the Living Your Dreams class. I started thinking about my dreams. One of my dreams was to find a husband; somebody I could love, and someone who could love me. That dream came true. God brought me a precious man, named John, to marry me and share the rest of my life with. I've never had someone like that in my life who loved me unconditionally. But God gave me a second chance at love.

This man did not come through the aid of her mother-in-law, for in this culture there are not typical kinsman-redeemers. I know of one story of a woman whose husband died, and by unusual circumstance, his brother fell in love with his former sister-in-law and married her.

In the case of Diane, we both prayed for a husband for her for years. She has maintained her relationship with her former mother-in-law all these years. It is a sweet relationship. But Diane and Felicia walked through challenging times as widows. Diane learned to depend upon God first and foremost in her life to get her through.

"After my first husband died, there were times when I was so upset, I'd be rinsing my daughter's diapers in the toilet and saying, 'I can't make it one more minute,'" but God gave me a second chance.

How very blessed we have been to have friends who love us, bless us, and share in our joys and sorrows. Marilyn and Bill Mitchell hosted our Hawaiian-themed wedding at their home on September 23, 2000. Marilyn was the minister who married us. We had 225 guests celebrating our new life with us. It was a dream come true! Our families, our friends, and our community surrounded us and shared in our joy!

Marilyn, Susie Dahlmann, and I had been in Bible Study for more than five years. In the past, I had felt intimidated by the Bible, but now it's come alive for me. Susie; Marilyn's daughter, Eron; and my daughter, Brienne, and I were baptized on May 31, 2003 in the lake near the Mitchell's home. It was such a precious and sacred blessing to be baptized. I received Jesus Christ as my Lord and Savior, and I was publicly surrounded by a community of believers. Our first mission trip to Nicaragua in December of 2003 was a life-changing step for my husband John and me. We were part of the leadership team for Mission Bridge, an introductory mission class taught at our church, Brighton Christian. In January 2005, we helped lead our second trip to minister on a short-term mission trip to Leon, Nicaragua.

Diane knows what it's like to "walk through the valley of the shadow of death" as David describes in Psalm 23. She, like Ruth, knows what it's like to go on in her life in spite of the pain that she has suffered. Yet, with God and a community of friends and family around her, including Felicia and her family, she has raised two beautiful daughters and found the new love of her life.

"If you are ever feeling devastated by life, feeling that you can't go on, and you have deep pain and deep sorrow, just put your trust in him. Give him your cares. Give him your worries. Give him your concerns. He will bring you through, and you will have the most wonderful life beyond your wildest imaginings."

Read the Book of Ruth, found nestled between Judges and 1 Samuel, in the Bible. It is four short chapters and a delightful story. Tell us something that you learned from this reading that you didn't know.

What do you think of the concept of a kinsman-redeemer and the design by the Israelite society to take care of widows and orphans?

For most widows and single-parent women today, there are no traditions to cover women in these situations. For many single-women parents in our culture, they must rely on their mothers and, in some cases, their fathers, to help take care of their families. But this is often a place of brokenness in our culture. Do you know someone in this situation? If so, how do they get through life?

Who is our kinsman-redeemer in modern times?

Diane would tell you that Jesus is her kinsman-redeemer and that she has ultimately been saved by the blood of the lamb. If you have not taken this step, it's all the difference between living life on your own, or with one who can redeem you and give you the hope that Diane now has. Some of us have taken this step, but in either case, write a prayer to Jesus to begin or renew your faith in him today.

As Diane said, "If you are ever feeling devastated by life and you can't go on, you have deep pain and deep sorrow, just put your trust in him. Give him your cares. Give him your worries. Give him your concerns. He will bring you through, and you will have the most wonderful life beyond your wildest imaginings."

We invite you to pray to the kinsman-redeemer, Jesus, right now.

NOTE: Please read your homework assignment for next week now. Notice that you have a letter to write to a woman who has inspired you in your walk with Jesus.

PRAYER REQUESTS:

NOTES:

Chapter 8: A Proverbs 31 Woman, You and a Mentor, too!

We've reached the final chapter of this study. No study of Old Testament women would be complete without studying the Proverbs 31 woman. Who is she and what do we know about her? We don't have a name for her, and it's written in the section of the book of Proverbs by Solomon, as the Sayings of King Lemuel, an oracle his mother taught him. What we don't know is if this is one woman being described or several virtuous characteristics of women. This historical piece is not made available to us as far as I know.

Before you go any further, read Proverbs 31:10–31. In preparation for this chapter, I did an Internet search on the Proverbs 31 woman. There was everything from studies to raise your daughter in more virtuous ways to commentaries of women who questioned how there can possibly be this kind of superwoman. We do know this: it's been studied over and over again by women seeking to be mentored by this Old Testament super heroine and her great virtues. So today, we'll take a crack at what it might mean for us.

What do we glean from this woman? We know that a "wife of noble character" is considered "worth more than rubies" (Prov. 31:10). "Her husband has full confidence in her" (Prov. 31:11).

Consider that this Proverb of wisdom is included in King Solomon's writings. In 1 Kings 11:3, it says that Solomon "had seven hundred wives of royal birth and three hundred concubines (mistresses), and that his wives led him astray."

One can only imagine that Solomon had multiple experiences of virtuous and not-so-virtuous women along the way. So perhaps he found a blessing from these thoughts of King Lemuel's mother, wrote them down, and posted them on the walls of the palaces where he housed all these women. We'll never know.

We do know that this Proverb has stood the test of time to inspire us as women to be virtuous in the best way that we can.

In the next verse, it says that, "She brings him good, not harm, ALL THE DAYS OF HER LIFE!" (Prov. 31:12). This must have been a godly woman. We know that she is crafty in the good sense!

I remember years ago when we had a neighborhood Christmas party and I was working full-time. I met a neighbor woman who asked me what crafts I liked to do. At the time, I was building the craft of being a business woman, and helping to provide for our family. There was little time for knitting or sewing. But this Proverb woman's craftiness was part of survival as she "selects wool and flax and works with eager hands" (Prov. 31:13). These materials were needed for everyday clothing. She is the "Martha Stewart" of her home. She gets up early to "provide food for her family" and even "for her servant girls" (Prov. 31:15). We do know that fast food was not part of this culture and that everything was "homemade," but she did have help from the servant girls. We see that she is disciplined to get up early to prepare for her family.

A few years ago, I was asked to speak at the bridal shower of a friend's daughter. I rewrote Proverbs 31, describing the virtues that this young new wife might have in modern times. At the time, this young woman planned to work and utilize her business degree. So when we read that the Proverbs 31 woman "considers a field and buys it, and out of her earnings she plants a vineyard" (Proverbs 31:16), we see that this is not a stay-at-home mom who is not allowed to work outside of the home. She's an Old Testament career woman! We see that she is wise concerning business matters.

Next, we hear that "her arms are strong for her tasks" as she "sets about her work VIGOROUSLY!" (Proverbs 31:17). No having to lift weights for her or attending aerobics classes. She likely has gotten strong from her work. This is not your standard "girly girl." Not only does she get up early, she works late and she burns the midnight oil as well. This is no slacker. She is a "profitable" "trader" (Proverbs 31:18). We have no idea what she is trading, but certainly it is something that is needed for her family.

Again, we see that she works with her hands, preparing yarns and threads to make clothing (Proverbs: 31:19). We see that she has the gift of mercy and that she "opens her arms to the poor and extends her hands to the needy" (Proverbs 31: 20). Like Michigan where I live, it snows where she lives, and her family is covered in "scarlet" clothing. She even makes the coverings for her own bed. No going to Bed Bath & Beyond or to the outlets for sheets and blankets. She weaves her own (hopefully with the help of the servant girls). Moreover, she is dressed "in fine linen and purple" (Proverbs 31:22). Purple is such a royal color. Perhaps she was one of the original Red Hat Club women who wear the color purple.

Her husband has a fine position as a leader in their community because he sits at the "city gate," where important decisions are made. She has a cottage industry with her "linen garments" and "sells them" (Proverbs 31:24). So much of what we've heard about her has to do with providing for her family with clothing and food—the basics of life. Now we learn even more about her character. "She is clothed with STRENGTH and DIGNITY" (Proverbs 31:25). And she has a sense of humor for the days ahead. She "speaks with wisdom, and faithful instruction is on her tongue" (Proverbs 31:26). This is a point that we will come back to again.

As "she watches over the affairs of her household," she does the low-carb thing and "does not eat the bread of idleness" (Proverbs 31:27). No soap operas for this woman! "Her children arise and call her blessed, her husband also, and he praises her" (Proverbs 31:28). She is a woman who surpasses "them all" (Proverbs 31:29). We don't know if she is charming or beautiful, but we do know that she is a godly woman "who fears the Lord" (Proverbs 31:30). Finally, we see that she is "rewarded" and that "her works bring her praise at the city gate" (Proverbs 31:31), where all the men who are elders sit and discuss important matters.

Certainly, she is an inspiration to us. Perhaps we don't know who of us fits the bill in all of these areas of noble character, confidence of her husband in her, bringing good at all times, a good craftswoman, leader, trader, provides food, handles a staff, is disciplined to get up early and stay up late, she's merciful to those is need, she has a good sense of color and warm clothing and is dressed royally; she's the wife of a noble man, a leader, has dignity and wisdom, gives good counsel, is certainly not lazy, she is blessed and praised by husband and children; as a godly woman, she "fears the Lord, and she is rewarded for her virtue." Wow, what a woman! It's remarkable that one woman could have so many virtues.

At this stage, we're going to take a different approach. First, each of us has some, if not all, of these virtues or other ones that fit best for us. Glance over the list in the last paragraph and see which ones fit for you. Circle the ones that you might have. Then answer this question: what other virtues or skills do you have that are not listed here? List them. Take a stretch and look at your strengths!

What is an area of your life where you would like to grow in virtue and strength?

One area that I'd like to point out from the Proverbs 31 woman is that she "speaks with wisdom and faithful instruction is on her tongue" (Proverbs 31:26). This woman was likely a mentor to other women—young and old alike. She seemed to have a good grasp on life, but we see that she was willing to share what she knew with others. All of us have had women mentors in our lives, whether in passing or in a structured setting. First, think of a woman who has been a mentor, especially in your faith walk with God in your growing years. All of our years are hopefully growing years. Second, Diane Dorcey suggests that we take the time to honor our mentor by writing her a letter. Perhaps you have lost contact with this woman or she is deceased, but it's still a valuable exercise. In this letter, you want to let this woman know what attributes, characteristics, or virtues she had that you admire in her. Specifically, think of ways that this woman encouraged you to walk closer to God, especially in a challenging time. You can share specific ways that she has impacted you by citing examples. If the woman is living, you will write the letter to send to her. You may have more than one person that you'd like to send a letter to. You are more than welcome to do that. What we do ask is that you come prepared to share what this experience was like for you. Write some notes here about what this was like for you.

An additional thought is that you may be one of those women mentors for someone else. Can you recall a time during which you impacted the life of another woman and she was encouraged by you?

Part of our purpose of this study is to help us grow stronger in our own faith in God. Also, as we grow in our faith, we will be "bearing fruit for the kingdom" as we die to self and God lives in us. As a result, we will impact others with wisdom, kindness, love, gentleness, discernment, mercy, understanding, knowledge, and insight, all at the hand of a loving Father God and his son, Jesus. Think of a young woman or girl that could gain value from you coming alongside them.

Now write a prayer to our loving God for that person and for the courage to walk alongside them in their time of growth or need. Include in it a prayer asking God to develop you in the area of your life where you want to develop greater strength.

Women's Stories for God's Glory
Group Feedback Sheet

Name: (optional)

What did you like best about this study?

What did you learn about your walk with God through this study?

We value your honest (gentle) feedback. How could we have improved this study?

What stories of women from the Old Testament did you like best?

LEADER'S GUIDE

The following information will assist you as the leader of this study.

Ideally, the group will consist of eight women in addition to you. If you have fewer or more women, the structure of the session needs to be adjusted to accommodate this. In addition, it may be done in a large group setting, but it will need to be divided into groups of eight for the group discussion portion.

I suggest that you may want to have an Information Session before you launch into the eight-week study. In this session, participants will receive the book and a general overview of the study will take place. This can also be an opportunity to get to know one another. You may conduct this session to fit your particular group needs, or you can follow this format.

Sign-in/registration takes place first with all the pertinent information—name, address, city, zip, best phone number, e-mail address, kids, and childcare needs if you are offering childcare. I also prepare a light, healthy snack and beverages.

I pair women together and then I instruct them to ask this series of questions of each other: tell me your name, how long you have been at this church (if pertinent), something about yourself, and what drew you to this study, and what you would like to accomplish in this program. Each person will share with a partner for two minutes each, and then with the whole group. I, as the instructor, take notes on what I have heard for future reference. In the last half hour of the session, I will share my story of my lifeline as it relates to my walk with God. This is done in fifteen to twenty minutes. I am modeling for the participants how they will do this in the following weeks. Each leader will share her personal story to provide an example. I pass out a sign-up sheet. Each person signs up to tell her story for a particular week, and she also brings a snack for that session as well. The homework for the first week is to read and complete the questions for session one prior to that session.

Session one and those beyond will have this format:

Welcome/Greeting/Opening Prayer. After this, I read the pertinent first-person story of the character(s) for that week (included at the end of this section). The participants are asked to close their eyes as I read the story for that week. It is a great way to transition from their active lives and prepare for the evening.

After that, we review the lesson, making sure to be interactive to answer questions and hear any comments or insights. Saving the last half hour at the end of the session, we spend the remainder of the time answering the questions at the end of the lesson. This is usually a rousing session. I don't force all to speak, but I encourage those we haven't heard from to participate. Typically, those who are more extroverted will dominate the discussion, and as a leader, I attempt to include *all* in the discussions. Sometimes I will take a particular question and have the participants pair up and answer the question. Then I will ask them what they heard or discovered that was interesting. This creates a different dynamic, and the women seem to appreciate this.

Finally, the woman who has signed up to share her story that week will present. Typically, we get a snack prior to this. I usually let the presenter share without interrupting. At times, she may need encouragement, or she may need me to ask a question to bring out more of her story. Depending on the session, we will end in prayer, and we often take prayer requests that we encourage the other women to write in their Prayer Requests section of that session to pray about throughout the week. A bond is being built session by session for these women. I recall hearing about a group of women that participated in the *Women's Stories for God's Glory* study seeing each other at a church service, hugging, and celebrating that they knew one another. The women often share prayer request needs after the study is complete.

Please feel free to e-mail me at marilyn@wsgg.org if you have any questions about leadership of this study.

The following are stories that coincide with each session—to be read as the women have their eyes closed.

SESSION ONE: EVE'S STORY

I am the first woman—Eve. I was not born from a womb of another woman, but created by God out of the rib of Adam, the first man and my husband. When God created Adam, he saw that Adam was alone and he said that it was not good for him to be alone. He had put Adam into the most beautiful garden that you've ever seen. God had made it with beautiful plants that were also good to eat and streams, and rivers of water. God had told Adam that he was free to eat from any tree in the Garden of Eden, but he said to Adam, "You must not eat from the tree of the knowledge of good and evil, for when you eat of it you will surely die" (Gen. 2:17). When God had made birds of the air and beasts of the field, he brought them to Adam to name them. But God said that Adam needed a suitable helper. When Adam was asleep one night, God took one of his ribs and made me, the first woman.

Adam said, "This is now bone of my bone and flesh of my flesh; she shall be called woman or Adamah, for she was taken out of man" (Gen. 2:23). We were naked in the garden, but we were not ashamed. It seemed so natural for us. We were blessed beyond belief. God made us both in his image.

Then along came a serpent, as we were near the tree that God had told Adam not to touch. That serpent got me into trouble. He made me question why God would not want me to even touch it. Later, I realized God had never said not to touch the tree, but not to eat its fruit. That sly snake got me into trouble. He said that if I ate the fruit it would open my eyes and that I would be "like God knowing good and evil" (Gen. 3:5). But I was the one who actually ate the fruit. Then I gave it to Adam, who was with me at the time, and he ate it too.

Well, it did open our eyes. We saw that we were naked, and we covered ourselves with fig leaves. Then we heard God coming, and we hid from him because we were naked and afraid. When God questioned us, Adam blamed me and I blamed the snake. God told the snake, the evil one, that he would be cursed of all the animals, and that I, my offspring, and the snake's offspring would be enemies. God told us that because of what we had done we would be cursed. I would have pain in childbirth, and I'd desire Adam and he'd rule over me. He told Adam that he'd be working hard to provide food for us, when it had been so abundant for us before.

The Lord killed the first animal to provide clothes for us to cover our nakedness. Then he set us out of the garden.

Oh, why did we disobey God? Life was so good. Why did we ever get near that tree? What were we thinking? God joined us together for good, that we would be one flesh. We were the first married couple living in paradise. Now we labored to live. God just wanted to be in relationship with us, and we blew it. We had two sons, and the curse carried on when our son, Cain, killed his brother, Abel. Cain was cursed to wander all the days of his life. We then gave birth to Seth. Through his lineage, Noah was born one day.

If I could go back, I would have never eaten that fruit. I would have obeyed God. Now I will forever have the mark of the first human who sinned.

SESSION TWO: SARAH'S STORY

I am Sarah. Well, actually I was born Sarai, meaning Princess, and I became the wife of Abram, who became Abraham, the father of the nation of Israel. Most people are nearing the ends of their lives at sixty-five. For my husband and me, it was the beginning of a journey to travel to a place we had never been, to Canaan, south of where we had lived in Haran. We had moved because my husband had received a call from God to go from our homeland to a distant place. The Lord told Abram that he would make a great nation from him and that all the people on earth would be blessed because of him.

When we got to the land of the Canaanites, God promised to give Abram's future offspring this land. It was hard to establish a life there because of drought, so we left on a journey to Egypt. Some say that I was a beautiful woman, and my husband, Abram, was concerned that Pharaoh would kill him and take me away from him. So Abram convinced me to join him in the deception of Pharaoh by saying that I was his sister and not his wife. I was taken into Pharaoh's palace, and when serious diseases struck the people in his home, Pharaoh challenged Abram to tell the truth.

We were sent on our way. I continued to age, yet I had no children. I gave my maidservant from Egypt, Hagar, to Abram so that she could bear children for him. I didn't trust that the Lord would fulfill his promise to make a great nation through me, too. When Hagar became pregnant, I began to despise her. With Abram's permission, I mistreated her. She fled from us, but in time, she came back and gave birth to Ishmael, Abram's first son, when he was eighty-six.

Then, God made a deep covenant with my husband, and our names were changed. He became Abraham, which means "father of many," and I became Sarah, still meaning princess. God told Abraham that He would bless me with a son at the age of ninety! Imagine that! He would name him Isaac. I overheard three men of God talking with Abraham, and I laughed to think that I would have a child long past my childbearing years. How could this be? Only a supernatural act of God would do this for sure!

Yet I did have a son, and he is named Isaac, which means "he laughs." Both Abraham and I laughed to think that God could give us a son so late in life. Take the oldest woman that you know—someone in their 80s or 90s—and imagine them giving birth to a child. That God, when he does something, he does it in a supernatural way!

SESSION THREE: REBEKAH, LEAH, AND RACHEL'S STORIES

I'm Rebekah, the granddaughter of Nahor and the wife of Isaac. I was brought to my husband, having never met him, by his father Abraham's servant. Imagine that! I had never seen him before, and I entered a life that I had never known. I, like my mother-in-law, Sarah, was barren for twenty years. Then, joy of joys, I gave birth to twins, Esau and Jacob. When I was pregnant, I heard this word from the Lord, "Two nations are in your womb, and two peoples from within you will be separated: one people will be stronger than the other, and the older will serve the younger" (Gen. 25:23). Although Esau was the firstborn, I favored Jacob and helped him in deceiving my husband, Isaac, when he was old. Jacob fooled Isaac and received his blessing to become the heir of his wealth. Esau held a grudge against Jacob for stealing his birthright. I beckoned my husband to send Jacob to get a wife from my brother Laban's family.

I am Rachel, Laban's daughter. Jacob came to us to find a wife, and he fell in love with me, although I have an older sister, Leah. My father promised Jacob that if he would work for our family for seven years, he would give me to Jacob as a wife. But my father tricked him and gave my sister, Leah, to him. Then, a week later, I became his wife. Jacob loved me more. But I was barren and unable to bear sons for my husband.

I am Leah, the unloved one, Rachel's older sister. When God saw that I was unloved by Jacob, he blessed my womb and gave me six sons and one daughter. My servant, Zilpah, also gave my husband two sons.

I, Rachel, gave my servant, Bilhah, to Jacob, and he blessed us with two sons. In time, God heard my prayers and opened my womb. I gave birth to Joseph, the most highly favored of his father, Jacob. I became pregnant one more time. I died as I gave birth to my son, Ben-Oni. My husband named him Benjamin in the end.

We are the mothers of the twelve tribes of Israel, the name that the Lord God gave to Jacob—Reuben, Simeon, Levi, Judah, Issachar, Zebulun, Gad, Asher, Dan, Naphtali, Joseph, and Benjamin.

I am Leah. It is my son Judah whose lineage gave birth to Jesus—the Lion of Judah—so many generations later!

SESSION FOUR: RAHAB'S STORY

I am Rahab. I live in Jericho. I have one of the oldest professions of women, for I am a prostitute. I know, you look down on me for what I've done. You don't know how many times I've felt shame as I've walked through the streets of Jericho. I would often cover my head and face to avoid the stares of other women.

But I have been exposed to men who traveled with their caravans past the walls of Jericho, and they would visit with me in my home nestled in the city wall. I have heard many things about different people over the years. But I have recently heard the most startling stories of a people called the Israelites. I was told that they were God's chosen people and that he took them out of slavery in Egypt. He even parted the Red Sea so that they could cross over, and Pharaoh and his soldiers in chariots perished. They had been in the desert for forty years, preparing to take the land flowing with milk and honey. Their God had promised it to them. I'd also heard how God had given them victory over the two kings of the Amorites—Sihon and Og. The men I had heard speaking expressed fear that their new leader, Joshua, the son of Nun, would certainly wipe us out.

Then one day two men came to spy on my people, and I hid them on the roof of my house under stalks of flax. The king sent someone to ask me where these men were, and I lied. You see, I had my family to protect. I had more wisdom than most people thought I did. I told the messenger from the king that the men had gone on their way outside the high city walls. These men told me to gather all my family, collect them inside my home, and hang a red cord in the window on the side of the house where I let these men down.

I watched anxiously as seven priests walked around Jericho. Would we be saved? Or would some worse fate await us? After all, I had not led a very good life. But I did love my family and wanted to save their lives. After they had circled for seven days and those rams' horns sounded, the walls of Jericho tumbled down. Our family was saved. But even more so, I was saved by the God of the Israelites.

I became a wife of Salmon, and the mother of Boaz, the same Boaz who took Ruth as his wife. It was through our line—the line of Judah—that King David was born, as eventually was Jesus, through his father, Joseph, although they say that he was conceived by the Spirit of God through Mary. Many years later, it is told that I was commended for the faith that I had displayed. I was the only woman commended in such a way—me, a prostitute! That God of Israel, he sure can change a woman's life! Wouldn't you agree?

SESSION FIVE: DEBORAH'S STORY

I am a mother of Israel. My husband's name is Lappidoth, and my name is Deborah. Some say that I am a prophetess, that I walk closely with the Lord, and that I hear his voice as he speaks to me. Over time, I have risen as a leader in my country. They call me a judge, and I settle disputes for the people under the Palm of Deborah between Ramah and Bethel. It was not a good time in our country. Although the law that came through Moses made it clear that we were not to follow the other gods of the people whose land we were given by the Lord, our people didn't listen. Although so many had turned from the Lord and did evil in the eyes of the Lord, I did my best to follow the Lord and his commands.

Some would ask why the Lord would allow a woman to be used by Him to speak to his people. I think that it was simple. He used me because I was willing to listen to him. Even when things got really bad for our people and for twenty years our people were oppressed by Sisera, the Lord spoke to me. Sisera was the commander of King Jabin and Canaan's army. Oh, it was a mighty army with nine hundred chariots, and the men with them constantly put pressure on us. There was nothing wrong with my listening to the voice of God. It was my highest pleasure. I worked diligently to hear his voice to settle the disputes among the people of our land as a judge. But more than anything, I never ceased to thrill at the fact that the Lord wanted to speak through me. I have always feared the Lord and honored what he called me to do as a mother of Israel.

The Lord told me to tell Barak, son of Abinoam, to take ten thousand men from the tribes of Naphtali and Zebulun, and to lead the way to Mount Tabor. I did that. I also told Barak that the Lord would hand Sisera and his troops and chariots into his hands. Even then, Barak would only go if I would go. I told him then that the honor would not be his, but that the Lord would hand Sisera into the hands of a woman. That's just what he did. First, as Sisera led his men into the dry Kishon Riverbed, the Lord sent thunderous rains, and the men in their chariots sank into the mud. Our men took charge and defeated Sisera's men. Then, another woman, Jael, not from our tribe, hid Sisera in her tent. She drove a stake through his temple and put him to death. The victory for this battle was a woman's.

I was made for this time, but I have great pleasure in the Lord that he would use me—a handmaiden of the Lord and a mother of Israel. Oh, our Lord is so good, and his mercy endures forever and ever more. May his name be praised in all the earth!

SESSION SIX: ABIGAIL'S STORY

I am Abigail. Few people know about me. I was the wife of Nabal, a man of great wealth in Carmel, near the desert of Maon. We wanted for nothing with one thousand goats and three thousand sheep, but my husband was mean and surly in his dealings with others. Some say that I am beautiful and intelligent, too.

David, the one who would be king one day, sent ten young men to Nabal to seek supplies for him and his men. They were fleeing King Saul and had little, and that Nabal acted as a fool. David had protected our sheep during the time of shearing, and we had prospered as a result, but Nabal didn't care. He sent the men away empty handed. The fool! Didn't he know that David would return with hundreds of his men to attack us and take everything we had?

When my servant told me what had happened and how Nabal had hurled insults at David's men, I knew that something must be done for the goodness he had shown us. I lost no time in gathering two hundred loaves of bread, two skins of wine, five dressed sheep, roasted grain, and hundreds of cakes of pressed figs, and raisins. With my servants, we loaded the provisions onto the donkeys. I didn't tell my husband, Nabal, and perhaps I was disobedient in this, but I had to save our lives.

We rode to where David and his men were located. When I saw David coming toward us, I fell at his feet and put my face to the ground in humility. I asked that the blame be on me alone—that he pay no attention to Nabal, foolish though he was. I presented the gifts of food to them and asked forgiveness of David. The Lord revealed to me that David was his servant and that he had fought the Lord's battle; the Lord would make a lasting dynasty from him. I was told that he would favor David and would one day make him leader of all Israel. I asked that when David, my master, had received success from the Lord, he would remember me, his servant. I humbled myself that day in the presence of God's chosen one.

David blessed me for my good judgment. He received my offering and sent me home in peace. Nabal was holding a banquet when I returned, and he was drunk. I waited until the morning to tell him what had happened. Nabal's heart failed him and he became like stone. Ten days later, Nabal died. I was free. David sent word to me requesting that I become his third wife. I was delighted to be the wife of a man so favored by the Lord. In the end, I was blessed by the Lord for my wisdom and resourcefulness.

SESSION SEVEN: NAOMI AND RUTH'S STORY

I am Naomi, an Israelite woman. I married a man of fine standing in my tribe, Elimelech, and we made our home in Bethlehem. When famine hit, we moved to Moab, where we could provide food for our two sons, Mahlon and Kilion. Then disaster struck and my husband, Elimelech, died. As I mourned my loss, we didn't go back to Bethlehem, but my sons took wives from the Moabite people—Orpah and Ruth. We stayed for ten years, and then a worse disaster struck when Mahlon and Kilion died. I thought that my life had ended. I spoke to my daughters-in-law and encouraged them to go back to their mother's homes. I told them that I would go back to Bethlehem, the land of my people. Orpah wept and hugged me goodbye, but Ruth, the blessed girl, would not go home. She wanted to come with me.

Ruth said, "Where you go I will go, and where you stay I will stay. Your people will be my people and your God my God. Where you die, I will die and there I will be buried." Then she said, "May the Lord deal with me, be it ever severely, if anything but death separates you and me." (Ruth 1:16-17)

Who has ever had such a daughter-in-law? I was bitter, and when I returned to my people, the women asked if this could be me, Naomi. I beckoned them not to call me by my name anymore, but by Mara, which means bitter, for I had lost a husband, two sons, and a daughter-in-law. I had not much hope for the future. But Ruth, she was resourceful. She went to glean barley in the field of one of my husband's relatives, Boaz. He took good care of her, and I hatched a plan to seek him out as a kinsman-redeemer. We were both widows. I had no hope to give Ruth another husband, but God had another plan for us.

I told Ruth to prepare herself with her best clothes and perfumes and to go to the threshing floor, where Boaz would be. I gave her instruction to uncover his feet and lie there on the floor. I told her that he would guide her as to what he might do to redeem her. Everything went as planned. Today, Ruth has a husband and I have a son—well, a grandson—but Ruth and Boaz provided me with an heir for my husband and son. How good our God is!

I am Ruth. You have heard the story of what I have walked through and how I have followed my mother-in-law into a land I didn't know and a people I barely knew. It was frightening to go there, but I followed Naomi's God and not the gods of my people. He led me to the field of a man, Boaz, who was called a kinsman-redeemer. I was blessed as he protected me and gave me water and food to eat. I followed all of Naomi's wisdom and prepared myself to approach Boaz on the threshing floor. How my heart fluttered as I approached him. I had never done such a thing. But God protected me again. Boaz told me that he would approach a closer relative first to see if he wanted to redeem us. He sent me home to Naomi with handfuls of barley in my apron. It was not to be that the other would redeem me.

Oh, how I wish I could have been a fly on the wall to watch how Boaz took responsibility for Naomi and me and the land belonging to my father-in-law. It all unfolded as such a blessing for us. I became the wife of Boaz. I conceived and bore him Obed, a son for me and a son for Naomi; someday a grandfather of the future King David. Who would have foreseen such an outcome? Only God knew how it would play out all along. What if I hadn't followed the leading to go with Naomi? It all would have been different! Oh, I am blessed because of the God of Israel, who showed his favor upon me, a Moabite woman. How blessed I am.

SESSION EIGHT: THE PROVERBS 31 WOMAN: A MODERN-DAY VERSION

Where can we find a wife of great character today?

She is worth more than all the diamonds in the world!

Her husband has total confidence in her, and she lacks nothing in value!

She is the bearer of good things, not bad things, all the days of her life.

She knits acrylic hats and scarves for the orphans in Guatemala.

Her hands fly across the needles of brightly colored yarn.

She shops at Costco, Sam's Club, and Wal-mart, finding gourmet foods for her family to feast on from far-off places like Thailand, Japan, and India.

She's up before the crack of dawn, pulling out breakfast bars and hard-boiled eggs. She makes coffee and bagels to feed her family.

She searches out real estate that she can invest in, which will yield good earnings in the future.

She does her devotions and praises the Lord before she jumps into her day.

She sets about her work for the day, but not before she has done her workout, strengthening her arms with her weights.

She is a successful business woman, trading on eBay for the things that she needs for her house and family.

She is often burning the midnight oil as she answers her e-mail and keeps in touch with the world of people she knows.

She always opens her arms to the poor and homeless, and extends her hands to those in need.

When it snows, she doesn't fear, for she orders long underwear from Eddie Bauer and makes sure that everyone has a down jacket from Lands' End to deal with the below-zero temperatures.

She goes to Bed Bath & Beyond and gets coverings for her beds so they are extra toasty at night when the chill is the greatest.

She goes to Kohls to buy flowing, comfortable, yet stylish clothes in bright colors like purple.

Her husband is respected by the elders of the church for all that he contributes to the body of Christ.

She goes to the farmer's market and sells crafts and clothes that she has made. Her fun fur scarves sell well, even to the other merchants.

She is clothed with strength and dignity, and she has a sense of humor that would have put Erma Bombeck to shame.

She speaks with great wisdom, having learned a lot from experience. She is a mentor to others and gives them faith-filled guidance.

She watches her home like a hawk and never sits eating nachos while watching soap operas.

Her husband and children sing her praises, and they call her blessed.

He says, "Honey, you are the greatest wife a man could have!"

She is not superficial, and even though pretty, she doesn't spend a lot of time looking in the mirror.

She fixes her eyes on Jesus, and to God she gives the glory!

She deserves to be rewarded for a life well lived, and may she be blessed all the days of her life!

Look for these follow-up studies by Marilyn Mitchell.

Women's Stories for God's Glory, Book Two. This is the second eight-week study in this series, based on the stories of women of the New Testament and contemporary women of faith. Each participant will share the story of how God has used her talents in the past and present.

Living Your Dreams (with co-author Diane Dorcey) is a course in following God's will for your life! This is an eight-week study designed to help participants to determine God's path for their lives.

Healing the Wounds of Your Past Religious Experiences is a study designed to assist those who have had potentially abusive situations emerge as they have attempted to follow God.

Printed in the United States
by Baker & Taylor Publisher Services